T0167923

What Is Happy Science?

IRH Press

BOOKS
IRH PRESS
New York

ISBN 13: 978-1-942125-99-0
Cover Image: Studiotan/Shutterstock.com
BestPix/Shutterstock.com

Printed in Canada

First Edition

BEST SELECTION OF RYUHO OKAWA'S EARLY LECTURES

VOL. 1

What Is Happy Science?

EL CANTARE

Ryuho Okawa

IRH PRESS

Footsteps of Ryuho Okawa's early lectures

1989.3.5 — 1989.7.8

1989年 第1回第1部
幸福の科学講演会

Chapter One

The lecture in the morning on March 5, 1989

Changes of the Truth Civilization

(At Shibuya Public Hall)

From now on, the Truth shall begin the march of Light. (From Chapter One)

The venue crowded with many people

Chapter Two

The lecture in the afternoon on March 5, 1989

What Is Happy Science?

(At Shibuya Public Hall)

The audience of approx. 2,500 people who gathered at Shibuya Public Hall

Happy Science values making progress based on realism and sees this as our ideal.

(From Chapter Two)

Kyushu Welfare Public Hall

The lecture on March 19, 1989

The Discovery of Enlightenment

(At Kyushu Welfare Public Hall)

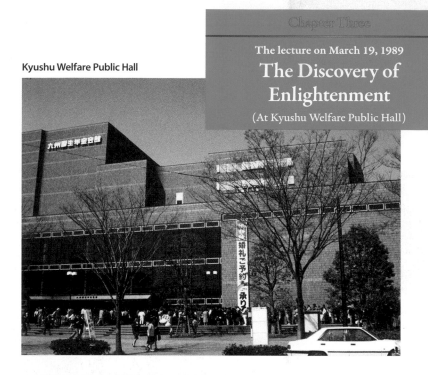

To discover enlightenment, you must first discover the "core" that lies within your own mind. (From Chapter Three)

The audience of approx. 2,200 people gathered at the venue

Kobe Port Island Hall

The lecture on May 28, 1989

Secrets of the Multidimensional Universe

(At Kobe Port Island Hall)

An electronic message
board in the venue

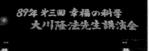

People lining up to purchase
new books and cassette tapes

An audience of approx. 4,000 people gathered at the venue

Please know just how
great a mission we
are expected to carry
out in this lifetime.
(From Chapter Four)

The ultimate self-realization means to live with God's Will as your own. (From Chapter Five)

The lecture on July 8, 1989

The Ultimate Self-Realization

(At Sonic City Large Hall)

Master Okawa gave a lecture to an audience of approx. 2,500 people, who gathered in the Large Hall

Contents

CHAPTER TWO

What Is Happy Science?

CHAPTER THREE

The Discovery of Enlightenment

CHAPTER FOUR

Secrets of the Multidimensional Universe

Preface

This book is a record of the lectures that I gave when I was 32 and 33 years old, in the second and third years after starting Happy Science.

It is a collection of my lectures that were given long ago—32 years ago, to be exact. However, the contents of the lectures have not grown out of date at all. These lectures could be called the study of human beings, philosophy, and the theory of the universe, and at the same time, an epic poem, spoken using modern words.

Looking back on myself, I may never give lectures like these ever again. So, I especially recommend that younger people in their 20s and 30s read this book.

I only had "passion" and "truth" as I gave these lectures.

Now, I have given 3,251 (3,500 as of June 2023) lectures. I shall leave no two footsteps alike. A young savior rose in Japan—I wish to hand down the events of those days as a record for humankind.

Ryuho Okawa
Master & CEO of Happy Science Group
January 9, 2021

CHAPTER ONE

Changes of the Truth Civilization

The First Public Lecture of 1989, Part 1

Originally recorded in Japanese on March 5, 1989
at Shibuya Public Hall in Tokyo, Japan
and later translated into English.

1

Beyond 3,000 Years of History

Thinking about the source of civilization

Thank you all for coming so early in the morning. I was very moved to see so many people lined up, even in this rainy weather. Seeing how earnestly you are seeking the Truth, I am filled with deep emotion as to how to respond to your passion.

We have two sessions today: one in the morning and one in the afternoon (see Chapter Two). This Shibuya Public Hall seats 2,500 people, which means there are only enough seats for Happy Science members. But I also wanted to welcome non-members to this rare opportunity, so I decided to hold two sessions in one day, despite the tight schedule.

My talks in the morning and in the afternoon will differ both in content and level. I have heard that there are non-members in the morning session, but my talk is mainly for members, so I will not go too easy on you [*laughs*]. Some topics are difficult to talk about in the presence of non-members, and I am usually reserved in my public lectures. But this morning, I will freely talk even if the topic gets a little eccentric or unbelievable.

The title of today's lecture is "Changes of the Truth Civilization." I wish I could talk about the history of 300–

400 million years, but that will take well over an hour, so I will focus on the more important parts. You probably know more or less how God's Laws that we are now seeking and exploring have flowed throughout the last 2,000–3,000 years. At one time, Moses was born in Egypt, and his teachings spread to Israel. Before that, Greek culture was at its height during the time of Zeus over 3,000 years ago and the time of Socrates over 2,000 years ago. About 2,000 years ago, Jesus was born in Israel and gave the teachings of love. Buddha taught the Truth in India 2,500–2,600 years ago. Around the same time, in China, Confucius gave his teachings, which are now called Confucianism. A little before that, Lao-tzu taught the philosophy that became the basis of Taoism. In the 7th century A.D., Muhammad gave the teachings of Islam. I am sure you have read about all this in my book, *The Golden Laws*.

However, I do not intend to talk about such recent history today. I want to go further back and share with you the source of civilization and the historical origin of Laws. There is no documentation left on the history beyond 4,000 years ago. There is no evidence left. I can only depend on my spiritual consciousness within me to see the history of humanity. So, there is no proof to confirm what I will be talking about. But the fact that you are living today means there were people who lived before you. If you think that the teachings of God were only given 2,000–3,000 years ago and never before that, then I have to say you have not thought enough about it.

The teachings of God have always been given. Although the teachings may differ in their form and appearance, spiritual leaders have always been born on earth in every age and have indicated a new direction. They taught how humans should think and advance. Their teachings were different depending on the age and region. Because of this, people who had learned the specific teachings or followed a specific stream of thought eventually could not understand why this difference existed. They tended to believe that their teaching was the only truth and that all others were heresy and false. However, I must say people feel this way because they have not been taught the truth and because those who learned the Laws did not deeply understand them.

Entering the great path of tolerance by knowing the Truth

Christianity that started in Israel has now spread to Western countries. And near Israel is Iran, where the teachings of Muhammad were given. You may have learned from newspapers and TV news that believers of Muhammad's teachings think differently from the people of Western countries. For example, Western people cannot understand

Ayatollah Khomeini's remarks at all. He says, "Blaspheming Muhammad deserves a death sentence," but the West cannot accept his statement. Western people cannot tolerate any blasphemy against Jesus Christ, but they do not care so much about blasphemy against Muhammad. However, now that you have gathered at Happy Science and learned the Truth that has been taught in a systematic and structured way, you will come to understand why people who have learned God's teachings think differently. Rather, you must be able to understand why. If you do not understand this, there would be no meaning to studying at Happy Science.

By knowing the Truth, we are entering the great path of tolerance. You are intolerant of others—namely, those who have different principles, opinions, or beliefs from yours— because you do not understand what their thoughts are founded on.

We, Happy Science, are now presenting different ways of thinking. By doing so, we are clarifying how each teaching was branched off, how the teachings should be classified, and how you should understand them. If you ever find the Light of Truth in an idea that is different from yours, you must respect it as a philosophy that manifests God's Light. Even if it is not yours, or even if it is an idea you cannot support, you must show respect toward it. We have adopted such an attitude. This is the true meaning of practicing the idea that "all religions have the same source." The idea is a beautiful concept, and I assume many people want to accept this idea. Many religious leaders may teach this. However, do they truly understand the real meaning of the idea that all religions have the same source? I doubt they have a sufficient answer. That is because they do not know the truth, the real fact.

Knowing the mere history of the last 2,000–3,000 years is not enough to truly understand that all religions have the same source. You have to look further back into ancient times and understand how human thoughts have been divided, how they have changed, and how they have manifested in response to the needs of each age. By looking at history, we need to learn what kinds of Laws are needed and how these Laws should be now, here, in this modern age.

2

Jesus' Unrevealed Past Lives
in Human History

(1) Clario, who was born in Egypt
more than 4,000 years ago

• The teachings of Clario

You may be familiar with Moses' teachings, but now I want to first talk about the teachings that were taught in Egypt before his time. More than 4,000 years ago, a man named Clario was born. He is one of the soul siblings of Jesus Christ. What did he do and teach in Egypt 4,000 years ago? Today, there are no documents left on this.

In those times, there were two pillars in the teachings that prevailed in Egyptian culture before Clario taught the Laws. One was the philosophy of reincarnation, which was already firmly established. As represented by the Egyptian pyramids, such as Pharaoh Khufu's pyramid, people in those times believed in reincarnation as a matter of course. This was a basic teaching, and almost no one doubted it. The second pillar was based on the underlying idea that human beings must face judgment upon death as they go through reincarnation. People believed that human beings face judgment upon death and are sorted into good and bad souls. The good souls come back after some time. That is to say, they are reborn in a human body and can be born into a higher class according to the level of their goodness. So, being born into a royal family was proof that the soul was noble. Then, what about the bad souls? The bad souls are first sent to a place called hell, where they experience severe ordeals. Through these ordeals, they are sorted into two types. One type is the souls who are never allowed to be reborn into this world. They will continuously be placed in the harsh conditions of hell and be burned eternally. The other type is the souls that still had a little goodness in them despite having fallen to hell. These souls can be reborn as animals that accord with their good tendencies. There were such ideas.

From the perspective of modern-day spiritualism, the idea of reincarnation, or the idea that judgment determines the next reincarnation, is 60–70 percent correct. But there are also misunderstandings—for example, the idea that the status of this world correlates with the spiritual grade of the souls and the idea that the bad souls either suffer eternally in hell or are reborn as animals. Of course, these are sometimes true, but there are also cases when souls rise to heaven from hell after repentance and are reborn as human beings. This idea was lacking in their teachings. But in those times, these were the mainstream beliefs in Egypt.

Then, what did Clario teach in this land of Egypt? He taught, "Whether you can be saved or not is not determined by the outcome of what you did. So, it is wrong to assume that committing a sin will automatically lead you to hell and that you will no longer be reborn as a human being. You are not judged by the results of your deeds alone. You are judged by your thoughts—what kind of thoughts? You are judged on how considerate you are of other people."

This was the same teaching of love he later gave as Jesus. Clario taught, "People who are more considerate of other people are good, whereas people who live selfishly are bad. After death, people are judged not by the sins that outwardly appear but by the kinds of thoughts they had throughout their lives. Thoughts such as how much love they had for others are important. So, even royal family members would suffer at the bottom of hell if they did not have any love to make their people's lives better and only lived for their desire for power and control. They are condemned for having built their own glory by suppressing the people, making them suffer, and imposing huge taxes and harsh labor."

Clario then said, "All of you, the spiritual grade of your souls is not determined by birth. The value of your souls is determined by the purity of your hearts. It does not matter even if you are born into a poor family, are born a slave, or are engaged in an occupation others do not respect. If your mind is close to God's Will, it means you were born and are living on earth on behalf of God; after leaving this world, you will be treated accordingly." This is what Clario, the past life of Jesus, taught.

Perhaps you can imagine how people reacted to this teaching. Of course, it was the greatest blessing ever for those who were oppressed and had no dreams or hopes in life. They thought, "We are in this situation by birth, so we thought we had no hope for the rest of our lives. But if our value is determined by what is in our minds and by our thoughts, then we have complete freedom over the world of our minds or thoughts. As Master Clario teaches, we have the freedom to control the kingdom of our minds. In this world, the king rules over us, but as for our minds, we, ourselves, are the masters who govern them." They were delighted by that and decided to follow this new teaching. People were overflowing with passion, and they gathered from different villages. As you can see, every time the soul of Jesus is born, he continues to pour his infinite love into the weak, the fragile, and the oppressed.

People fanatically gathered around Clario. Before long, they pushed Clario to be a leader, which he gradually became. People's passion became a tremendous force. People then urged Clario to be a new king and carried out activities to make it happen.

• The persecution by the ruling class

However, in those times, Egypt had an unbroken tradition of the royal family. How did this ruling class react? Perhaps it is not so difficult for you to imagine. Sure enough, they responded with severe persecution. Whenever they saw passionate activists who believed in Clario's teachings, they arrested them using military police-like forces. They dragged these activists away and placed them under forced labor, such as cutting and carrying stones to build the pyramids, in a remote area. People were sometimes buried alive as human sacrifices inside or under the pyramids. The ruling class repeated such brutal acts. People who believed in the teachings of Clario were taken away from their families, thrown into forced labor, and eventually killed. By doing so, the rulers tried to drive people's minds away from Clario's vibration of love.

But people in those times were strong, very strong. Why were they so strong? It was because they firmly believed in the eternity of the soul. People cannot be as strong when an increasing number of them do not believe in the eternity of the soul and live according to materialistic ideas, both of which can be seen in today's world. However, Clario's believers were strong. Even if they were not rewarded in this life, they believed in the world of eternity. To be precise, they *knew* it. They believed themselves to be a far greater being, not an insignificant existence dwelling in a body of an abused slave. And they carried their hopes over into their next lives.

No matter how hard the rulers persecuted or killed people, more and more of them came to support, believe in, and lay down their lives for Clario's teachings. Even the ruling class could do nothing to stop this movement. Clario then worked on establishing a new nation near the present-day Nile Valley in Egypt. It was a nation of believers of God's teachings, and he named it the "Kingdom of God." About 10,000 people came to live there and tried to create an ideal nation—the kingdom of souls. They developed a self-sufficient economy, and many took part in this experiment to create a new civilization under the guidance of Clario.

However, the end came unexpectedly for Clario and his people. Unfortunately, a betrayer appeared in Clario's new Kingdom of God, much like Judas in Jesus' time. As it happens in any age, the devil sneaked into the mind of one of Clario's disciples. And this devil inside invited the devil outside; the pharaoh's army launched a surprise attack on this new village. It was indeed a tragedy. They mercilessly killed the people, whether they were women or children. They used new weapons of those times. They used slings to throw large stones and shot fire arrows to set houses on fire. They then burst into the village with spears and swords. The pharaoh's army came with thousands of soldiers.

Villagers frantically ran about, trying to escape. They were usually vigilant, but because of the traitor, the pharaoh's army was able to attack when they were least on guard. The assault came the day before the festival celebrating the third anniversary of the founding of the new Kingdom of God. People were enjoying drinks on the eve of the festival, and security was weak with fewer soldiers on guard. People drank and sang in joy; it was a heavenly sight. Drunk and tired from dancing, they fell into a deep sleep without much security. Then, at midnight, the pharaoh's army launched a surprise attack, and the new village fell apart. Most villagers were massacred. Clario and a few hundred of his soldiers managed to flee upstream of the Nile River.

However, the pharaoh's army pursued them persistently. The fighting and chasing continued for about a month. In the end, Clario, together with some of his people and his beloved disciples, threw himself into the Nile River. He was 42 years old. It was a tragic life.

Two thousand years later, he was reborn in Israel as Jesus Christ. As you can see from this story, he lived the same kind of life again. Why does he lead such a life? Why does he experience a tragic end? It is because he chooses to be one with the oppressed and the sufferers. This attitude itself becomes a criticism against the establishment and shakes the rulers. His kind acts of love and his loving thoughts for the poor and the oppressed inevitably shake the ruling ideologies. Ultimately, such anti-establishment groups are always met with punishment from the ruling class. I am not saying all rulers are necessarily evil, but it is natural for them to take such measures.

This is how Jesus' soul lives. He lives with such a role. To realize a greater love, he removes his ego from his love and tries to become one with those he wants to save. This is how he always lives.

(2) Krishna, who was born in India about 7,000 years ago

• Aspiring to bring together love and politics

Clario's soul was born in India about 3,000 years prior to his birth in Egypt. He was born in Western India and was called Krishna. God Krishna is well-known in India. You may not know so much about him, but he also taught love.

Krishna was born a prince (I spoke according to what I received as spiritual revelations, although he is now handed down a little differently, as God of India). This time, Jesus' soul was born a prince. In those times, kingdoms in India were surrounded by many enemies, so he had to fight, although he did not like it. People lived in fear because their lives were always in danger. But much like in Egypt, people in India fully believed in the existence of the soul. They also fully believed in the concept of reincarnation.

What did he intend to do at that time? What was the aim of Jesus' soul, who was called God Krishna? In fact, he aspired to bring together love and politics. Unlike his later reincarnations, when he rose to fight for the weak, this time, he was in a political position, a ruling position, and tried to unite people under love.

Krishna took every measure to improve people's lives. He freed people of taxes and forced labor. He also tried to come up with a way to manage the army as efficiently as possible so that more people could live happily with their families. "How can I achieve it?" He thought long and hard about how to achieve this and came to a conclusion. He said to himself, "If many ordinary citizens are called to serve in the military, their wives and children will be very unhappy. So I'll call for the people who will dare to fight along with me to the very end."

He considered the soldiers his disciples. He told them, "If possible, I'd like you to stay single because you'll eventually have to stake your lives on fighting. I ask ordinary citizens to raise a family and make a loving home. As for us soldiers, we will stake our lives on protecting the kingdom. So those of you who agree with my ideas and teachings, come alone. Give up your life and come alone. Becoming my soldiers means you have already died. Your physical bodies should be used to protect this kingdom. Soldiers will make up less than 10 percent of the population. But for the happiness of over 90 percent of the people, please become the shields and the swords and abandon your lives with me." He raised voluntary soldiers in this way.

The soldiers pledged to become one with Krishna's will and to share their fate with him. They vowed to fight when Krishna fights and die when he dies. They had faith in Krishna. In this way, faith, politics, and the military were united.

Krishna wanted to avoid involving the general public in the wars as much as possible. So 7,000 years ago, in India, he used all his wisdom to create the modern military of its time. What was it like? He invented a vehicle, not like the ones we see today but something similar to a handcart. He then harnessed horses to pull it. He also put a wooden board in front of the vehicle and attached devices to shoot arrows. The vehicle was pulled by two horses or three for a larger one. In the front, it had a wall-like board with small windows through which arrows were shot. In the back of the vehicle was a sling, like the ones used in Egypt, as I mentioned earlier. The slings were made of leather rather than rubber. They could launch stones larger than the size of a fist as far as 330 yards. Krishna built chariots equipped with slings, bows, and arrows. It was a revolutionary invention for his time. He then formed a unit of about 500 chariots. He trained professional fighters mainly around the unit of chariots. When fighting, the unit of chariots went forward first and put the enemy into a rout. Then, the unit of spear fighters went forth, followed by the unit of sword fighters. Krishna launched a three-wave attack.

He took this approach to minimize casualties. He tried to intimidate his enemies at an early stage to make them retreat. In the modern context, it is a defense-oriented strategy. The idea was to quickly push back his intruders by showing his overwhelming power. That is why he thought of such an unconventional strategy.

• The attack by the allied neighboring kingdoms

However, Krishna's army was eventually defeated. How did it happen? His army was invincible, but his soldiers were obviously small in number. So the surrounding kingdoms thought of strategies to defeat the army of a small number of soldiers. They did not just want to take Krishna's land. Krishna's kingdom was truly an ideal world. People were happy and united under their tremendous admiration for Krishna. But his kingdom posed a great threat to the surrounding kingdoms. Why? One reason was that other kingdoms imposed heavy taxes and forced labor on their people. People were forced to do construction work, were deprived of money, and were arrested as political prisoners if they were suspected of something. Their families were torn apart. Those who did not obey were mercilessly executed. The kingdoms surrounding Krishna's were governed by fear.

This can be seen in any age, especially during the warring states period. Rule by fear often becomes the mainstream practice. The neighboring kingdoms were ruling their people by fear. However, Krishna tried to govern people by love. This was a great threat to the surrounding kingdoms. The royal families—the ruling class—became flustered. What if their people were to revolt and demand the same kind of rule? They were so afraid that they could not sleep.

That is why they decided to join forces to defeat Krishna. Five or six kingdoms formed an alliance to crush Krishna's kingdom at all costs. And they thought of a very dishonorable plan. What was this plan? First, one kingdom launched an attack on Krishna's kingdom to lure his army. Then, they retreated, and when Krishna's army started to retreat, they launched an attack again. By repeating this for three days, they drew his army away from his kingdom. Krishna's army had to fight with full force because its number was limited. Then, the allied forces of five other kingdoms intruded into his defenseless kingdom, where over 90 percent of the ordinary citizens were living happily. As the women and children ran about to escape, the enemy forces set fire to their houses to completely destroy the kingdom.

Upon hearing about the emergency, Krishna's army made its way back home but was met again by yet another raid from behind. They were attacked from both sides. Tens and hundreds of thousands of enemy forces attacked Krishna's fighters of just a few thousand from both the front and the rear. Krishna's men could hardly defend themselves, and in the end, they all died in the burning chariots set on fire by the allied enemies. I know how it actually all ended. They all died fighting. This story might be handed down in India as a folktale in a somewhat different form. But what I told you is a true story seen with the spiritual eye. The rule of love was defeated in real politics.

(3) Agasha, who was born as the King of Atlantis 11,000 years ago

• Religions, science, and politics in the age of Atlantis

Then, how about the age before that? About 11,000 years ago, in the age of Atlantis, the soul of Jesus was born under the name Agasha. He was the last king of Atlantis. Known to be a very wise king, Agasha was very considerate of his people, but he also had great enemies. Many people believed in the teachings of Agasha and revered him as a great king. But in those times, much like today, there were many religious groups, including traditional groups and new groups that were rapidly on the rise. Many of the newly established religious groups focused on developing spiritual powers and causing spiritual phenomena. They then insisted that those who can make spiritual phenomena happen or who have tremendous spiritual powers are truly great people and superhuman. The end of Atlantis was approaching, and people were leading decadent and corrupt lives.

As you may have read in my other books, Atlantis had a highly advanced scientific civilization; they had submarines and airships. Airships floated in the sky in those times as they do today and used solar energy as the driving force to propel themselves forward. Submarines were shaped like orcas and had small, pyramid-like dorsal fins that absorbed solar energy to drive themselves forward. This meant that the submarines in those times sometimes came up to the surface of the water like whales to absorb solar energy before going underwater again. The airships used solar energy to fly, so they did not fly on a rainy day like today.

The age of Atlantis was a highly advanced time in terms of scientific technology. People were also politically advanced and had adopted a form of democracy. So the last days of Atlantis were very similar to Japan today.

The souls who lived on earth in a physical body back then are now born in masses. Many who had been born in those times have been reborn in the U.S. and Japan today. Although souls can be reborn individually, they tend to be born in similar groups into a similar civilization in masses. The population is increasing today because many who were active at the end of Atlantis are wishing to be reborn, and many of them are reborn in the U.S. and Japan.

We live in a similar age as Atlantis. The souls that were born in Atlantis are now being tested to see if they can finish their soul training without making the same mistakes they did in Atlantis. This is one of the goals of their soul training. In an age of advanced scientific technology, politics, and economy, they are trying to teach or learn what true faith is and what the true path to God is. Many souls are reborn with these goals.

It is surprisingly easy to believe in God when you are poor or oppressed. Looking at history, you may often wonder why such tragedies happened, why people were so poor, or why there was so much hardship. You may wonder why God allowed such ages to exist. However, it is surprisingly easy for souls to believe in God in times of tragedy, difficulty, or poverty. Why? It is because people try to rely on something Great when they live in misfortune. They are willing to ask for help without arrogance or conceit. People living under difficult conditions and at the mercy of fate cannot live or have hopes and dreams without relying on something Great. That is why they turn to God.

People awaken to faith and strongly believe in God in an unfortunate age or in an age of war. People often learn about faith in those times. However, once they are free of such difficulties and are born into an age when they are financially and materialistically blessed or into a convenient age with advanced technologies, they tend to forget the faith they used to have in the poor and difficult environment they experienced in their past lives. And they gradually grow arrogant. This arrogance leads them to be decadent. They start thinking they can do anything, and they feel as if they have become God Himself.

Nowadays, people can travel to outer space on a spacecraft. The people of Atlantis did not get that far, but they believed they had conquered the world because they had airships to ride and fly. They felt that the entire world was in their hands and that they had become God on the earth. The consequence of all this was that people lived a life of indulgence and pleasure. In every age, whenever there is an abundance of food, a life of decadence mainly based on pleasure follows.

• Agasha's teachings on love and his end by the coup

In the age of Atlantis, like in the present age, many dubious religious groups emerged one after another—similar to how bamboo shoots rapidly grow after the rain. They deluded people into the world of the occult and tried to divert their minds from boredom.

There were different kinds of groups. To cite some typical examples, one group focused on the practice of levitation, which is currently attracting some people today. The group taught that people could find salvation and become supermen if they could float in the air.

Similar groups to this focused on psychokinesis, much like how the practice of spoon bending is popular today. There were many groups like this. When scientific technology advances and people become capable of doing anything, they tend to want to try something unusual. That is why some groups focused on causing supernatural phenomena.

Other than these, there were religious groups that supported going back to the times of their ancestors. They taught people to abandon everything and return to a simple life and formed groups like the modern-day hippies. They encouraged people to reject civilized life and abandon everything, and they lived in groups like hippies. They upheld faith in God of an extremely primitive form. By calling civilization evil, they tried to go back in time and lived simply, like primitive people. They regarded those enjoying civilized life as their enemies and attacked them like guerrillas. They threw stones or set fire by throwing firebomb-like things at the houses of key government officials and business executives. People gathered under such an ideology.

Healing illness was also popular. Like today, there were many diseases of civilization, and some groups attracted followers by healing people's illnesses.

Many religious groups were flourishing. So Great King Agasha taught, "The central teachings must always be the teachings of the mind and the teachings of love. All of you, awaken to love. Awaken to your mind."

Those who were fascinated by spiritual phenomena or outward appearances were not satisfied with Agasha's abstract teachings. They also grew very angry at how their groups were losing momentum and driven into a corner because of Agasha's words and actions. They found their way to the key government leaders and told them, "Agasha is being manipulated by the devil. He must be Satan. He criticizes us, although we are doing something so great. He doesn't deserve to be a king. We must kill him at any cost." A group of fanatics emerged and insisted on such things. The group gradually gained tremendous power in many fields, including in the political and business circles, and tried to oust the Agasha group.

Then, a coup d'état occurred. You can probably imagine the outcome of the coup, as it is the same in every case. Agasha and many others were killed. In those times, there was a place called Agasha Square. Atlantis was a large continent situated in the triangular area off the coasts of present-day Spain, Florida of the U.S., and Ecuador. Agasha Square was located in the capital of Atlantis, and Agasha gave lectures in front of many people there. During the coup, the rebels dug up this holy Agasha Square. They then captured the people of the Agasha group who practiced politics based on the right teachings and killed and buried them there. It was a horrible incident. Agasha was also caught and eventually killed. At that time, his son Amon II fled to Egypt on an airship. This was the start of the Egyptian civilization. Amon II was the model for the legendary Amon-Ra. Like him, some people fled to Egypt either by air or sea.

• **The similarity between the modern age and the final days of Atlantis**

Sadly, however, Atlantis was hit by natural disasters in parallel with this ominous move that began with the killing of the Agasha group. The evil thought energy emitted by the rebels triggered a huge negative reaction from the Earth Consciousness, and the proudly prospering continent of

Atlantis sank overnight. It was an unbelievable sight. Most residents had no way of escaping and simply drowned to death.

Nevertheless, sinking the continent was by no means God's wish. Great guiding spirits were born, yet they were persecuted and killed along with many other angels who were born. This evil thought energy cast darkness over the already clouded Atlantis and blocked God's Light. As a result, the continent sank into the ocean.

This has happened in every age, and it can happen even today. As the evil thought energy of living people grows, changes will occur on the surface of the earth. Earth on which we live is not a mere material but the physical body of a huge consciousness called the Earth Consciousness. Earth is the huge body that the consciousness uses. Earth itself is a physical body. Earth Consciousness is a great divine consciousness. What happens when this consciousness finds something unpleasant or an ailment on the surface of its body? Self-purification. Think about it. If you get lumps and bumps on your hands or feet, your body will naturally try to get rid of them. The Earth reacts in the same way. In the long run, this self-purification often manifests as natural disasters.

The modern age is a very similar time to the final days of Atlantis. We are living in an age similar to the time when Agasha lived. Will we repeat the same folly in this age? Or are we going to change our minds, learn from past mistakes, and do something to pave a new way? We are now expected to choose the right path.

3

The Truth Shall Begin the March of Light

So far, I have talked about the past lives of Jesus' soul. Looking at how he had lived as Agasha in the age of Atlantis, Krishna in India, Clario in Egypt, and Jesus in Nazareth, we can see no trace of him being attached to his earthly life. But the sad thing is that although such a great person was born, people let him die helplessly. We must think about what remained in the hearts of these people.

Christianity often teaches the sense of sin or the sin of humanity. This does not only apply to the Jews in Jerusalem in those days. The reason behind this teaching is the karma of humanity. In the ages of Clario, Krishna, and Agasha, Jesus always lived for the love of the people and acted on great love, but many people failed to understand that. What is worse, they even massacred many messengers of Love or messengers of Light. They committed the most shameful acts as human beings. We must understand this grave karma of humanity that lies behind the teaching of sin. It is a symbol or reflection of human karma. Jesus' soul always uses it to enlighten people.

As we live at the end of the 20th century, many natural disasters are forecasted to occur on a global scale in the coming age. And just like in the ancient ages, many messengers of Love or messengers of Light are born today. Will people easily kill them again? In this modern age, "killing" does not necessarily mean taking their lives. "Killing" may mean suppressing their speech, culturally dismissing them, or politically oppressing them.

Comparing the present age with the age of Atlantis, the biggest problem is that there is nothing on earth that supports those who teach the religious Truth. Isn't that true? Nonetheless, there are countless forces that try to restrict them. There are laws and other things that suppress them. The more determined such religious people become to live for the Truth, the more cold shoulders they will experience. Many people may consider them mad or crazy or may ridicule them. This is the "persecution" of the present day.

Some people regard religion as evil and laugh about it. They try to hinder faithful people who are living for the Truth with Right Mind from succeeding at work, demote them, drive them to resignation, or make them give up on realizing their goals. This kind of oppression exists in companies, governments, and other places. This is the modern-day persecution. As an organization of Truth, will we overcome it? Or will we let them continuously commit the evil they are not even aware of? The time is coming when we must draw a conclusion.

I hope many strong people
Will come forth from among you.

If you have learned from history
Yet still allow people to repeat
The same folly and brutality today,
Then what is the point of their soul training?
Why are humans reborn again and again
And live in a similar age?
If we only repeat the same mistakes,
How can humanity make progress?

Now is the time to stand resolutely against
The thoughts, ideas, and actions that hinder the Truth,
Which are prevailing in Japan and other advanced nations.
The Truth is Truth.
Everything must be integrated under the Truth.
Everything started from the Truth.
Everything must gather under God's Light.
All order and all values
Have flowed from this single source,
So all must serve this single source.
We must firmly and clearly establish this idea.

All of you, from now on,
Do not compromise.

From now on,
The Truth shall begin the march of Light.
Gather before me, follow my hand,
And go forward straightly without any hesitation.
That is the reason
You were born this time.

Please gather to me and take action.
Believe in me.
Do not doubt me.
Just go straightly, on and on.
Gather to this White Hand,
And start taking action.

We must never compromise.
I will uphold the truth as truth,
Light as light,
And what is right as right.
Let us work together.

CHAPTER TWO

What Is Happy Science?

The First Public Lecture of 1989, Part 2

Originally recorded in Japanese on March 5, 1989
at Shibuya Public Hall in Tokyo, Japan
and later translated into English.

1

Happy Science Is "Genuine-Oriented"

Explaining what Happy Science is for newcomers

Today, I have a "doubleheader"—a lecture in the morning (Chapter One) and a lecture in the afternoon. I think hundreds of you attended the morning session, but please forget about that. The lecture in the afternoon will be on a completely different topic, and it will make it difficult for me to give this talk if you expect a continuation from this morning. This lecture is intended for newcomers, so please do not think that I have become too easy on you.

Happy Science members have been studying the Truth for a year or so, so they are ahead in their understanding of the Truth. So far, I have published 65 books (as of the lecture). Many members have read all of them and have gained different ways of thinking from those who have not. At any rate, it is not easy for first-timers to understand my lectures catered to our members, so we plan to teach the Truth according to each person's level of understanding in our activities from now on.

I am giving two lectures on completely different topics in the two sessions today, and I believe this style will be reflected in the future activities of Happy Science. In fact, the teachings of Happy Science cover a large range of ideas. They extend from easy teachings to difficult teachings, and there are diverse teachings. So even those who have studied our teachings in detail may find it difficult to understand the differences in the thoughts I am presenting.

The other day, I published a book of the same title as today's lecture, *What Is Happy Science?* In the book, I described the eight basic pillars that I narrowed down from the basic teachings I had put forth in the first couple of years. But this book alone is not enough to gain a good understanding of Happy Science. So today, I will set aside the content of the book and take a different approach to what I think Happy Science is. I would also like to talk about how we will develop and the activities I want to do at Happy Science.

Now, it is March 1989. Exactly two years ago, in March, I gave my first public lecture at Ushigome Public Hall ("The Principle of Happiness," now compiled as Chapter One in *The Ten Principles from El Cantare Vol. I*), and about 400 people attended. It was a fine day, but because it snowed the day before, I was worried no one would make it. I was quite nervous, and I expected 100–200 people to come at best. I remember feeling very happy to see 400 people as I stood at the podium.

However, two years later, 5,000 people are here today. My audience has grown this rapidly. But during the last two years, we did not put much effort into gaining new members.

Rather, we were doing the opposite; we adopted an application system to accept new members. Before launching Happy Science, I had been publishing books with Chobunsha Co., and in my seventh book, *Spiritual Messages from Himiko*, I put in information about Happy Science at the end of the book. Then, our membership rapidly grew to a few hundred. But we did not have any staff members at the time, and I wanted us to start out slowly, so I did not want our membership to grow so rapidly [*laughs*]. To keep our membership growth between one-fourth and one-fifth of what it would naturally be, I adopted an application system the following year, in 1987. Moreover, you needed to have read over 10 books to join us, so I anticipated about 100 people to join per year, but even then, far more people came to join us.

Why did we limit our membership at the start of our activities? Let me begin by talking about my basic idea behind this. As the starting point, we wanted people to recognize the difference in the ways of thinking between us and others. The difference is that we are "genuine-oriented." In the field of spirituality, all sorts of things were rampant, including shabby ones and dubious ones. There was a tendency to palm off a lot of things of poor quality. Upon observing this, I, myself, strongly opposed working in such a field. I did not want to at all. I thought to myself, "I don't want to do the same kind of work as them. If I must start my own, I want to do things I can be satisfied with. I want those who study at Happy Science to be satisfied as well. I want them to say that their lives changed for the better." That is why I drew the line between us and others by seeking what is true and right.

We believe our teachings are not true and right if people do not change after joining and learning at Happy Science. That is the reason we uphold the concept, "Graduate School of Life." The term "graduate school" gives off a difficult impression and puts people off, so it accords with our stance. So we put up a sign that says, "Graduate School of Life, Happy Science." This means to say that once you come to Happy Science, you are expected to study. Unless you are serious about learning, you will not be able to keep up. We have adopted a very transparent management system that says, "If you wish to follow us, follow us. If you want to join us, join us. If you want to leave us, leave us."

Why did we adopt this approach? It is because if we want to truly change the world, the pursuit of our membership growth alone is not enough. Times are changing, and the world is seeking something deeper, something more valuable, and something of higher quality. In society, many religions are subjected to criticism, and there are many books focused on accusing religions of raising money. Why is this happening? Perhaps some religions are doing those things in reality, but the main point is that people judge religion as something vulgar and lowbrow. They have a biased view that people who come to religions are below average. This is their point. They believe, "People below average seek help from religions because they are helpless and want to clutch at straws. Religions attract such people and are taking money from the poor." I presume 80 percent of people in general think like this.

To counter this trend, I must firmly criticize it from the inside, not from the outside. By joining the field of spirituality and producing something of good quality, and by dint of its good content, we can surely criticize and change their activities from the inside. We can change the people gathering there. Of course, I am passionate about spreading the Truth far and wide, but I thought I had to create something wonderful, something that never existed before, as the first step of religious reform. I wanted to change the field of spirituality itself and silence criticisms through our activities. I thought about these things.

As I wrote in the book *The New Business Revolution*, works that are considered valuable or wonderful in this world have all stood the test of time. Only good things have remained after competition. In the business or academic world, people compete with each other to produce something valuable or wonderful. But this is not the case in the field of spirituality. In this field, each group creates its own "stronghold" or "absolute world," insisting that only its God, not God in any other group, is the Primordial God of the universe. These groups fail to gain the understanding of others and stick to their own creed. That is how they run their groups. They must change this attitude if they are to improve themselves. That is how I think. You will not be able to produce truly good things if you cannot withstand criticisms.

The characteristics of Happy Science members

Here is what we are trying to do: By producing things of high quality, we want to urge other religious groups to reform themselves. We are challenging them to see if they can gather equally high-level members like the ones at Happy Science. We are tacitly criticizing them in this way.

As we enter our third year, I feel this approach has had a great effect. People who have joined us from other groups found our members to be of unusually high or extremely high levels. You will see it if you interact with our members.

Why are they such high-level members? There are two reasons for this. One reason is that they are very serious and passionate about seeking the Truth. They are earnest and have no bad intentions. We encourage our members to explore Right Mind, and indeed, they are purehearted and serious.

The other reason is that we have a culture of encouraging each other to improve. This culture of friendly competition works to push up the level of each individual. I believe no other group in the field of spirituality has ever promoted "self-improvement" as strongly as we are doing now. This is the kind of organization I have created. Our membership has been increasing a lot, but our level has not dropped an inch; our members have inherited the culture of our early days. This is true no matter how large our membership grows. Members are making efforts to change themselves. And they are learning the Truth very seriously. We can observe such a culture.

Recently, we held a preliminary course, and many of our members participated in it. Until last year, we had the Discipleship Course that consisted of the Basic, Intermediate, and Advanced Courses, but because there were many participants, we decided to introduce a preliminary course as a prerequisite to the Basic Course. About 2,000 members took the course, and they had never taken our seminar before, which meant they were newly joined members. And I was surprised at the test results. The test was multiple-choice, and the average score of those 2,000 members was 93 out of 100. In addition, out of 2,000 people, 436 of them got full marks. It was incredible. The test was based on three books, Monthly Messages, booklets, and my lecture recordings. All our lecturers, including myself, were amazed to see that even new members were studying this hard. We took off our hats to them. Our lecturers were saying, "How can we teach such high-level members? We may have nothing to teach them. We could consider those who got full marks to have passed the Advanced Course automatically." I have not met our members in person, but all of them, including those living in the local areas, have a strong desire to learn.

Is there any group that can hold a difficult test based on their books, have 2,000 of their members take it, and produce an average score of 93? I doubt it. In fact, many university professors failed our test. They did not know that our members were so passionate. Those who did not take the test as a serious matter failed.

How can we explain this? What kind of group has been formed? I feel that some kind of change is occurring among those who have gathered at Happy Science. What is this change? Perhaps it is the result of their seeking a new value system.

Until now, people may have sought to enter a prestigious high school, university, or company. Perhaps they have made an effort to work at a job that pays a higher salary. But how can we explain the passion of these thousands of people who have become members of Happy Science? What merit do they have in studying the Truth? To be honest, there is no merit in the worldly sense. Getting good marks on our tests will not bring them anything; it is no use elsewhere. They are simply confirming their understanding of the Laws. This means that more people are taking pleasure in studying and mastering the Laws. I find this a curious trend of the times.

In the past, anything related to religion was considered weird or suspicious. Or it was seen as a gathering of people who were below average or who were desperately seeking help. But as you can see, those who have gathered at Happy Science have a high level of intellect. They are sound people. I doubt those with mental disorders can get such high scores. Those who wholly depend on Other-Power probably cannot get good scores. This is proof that Happy Science is a group of people who are determined to carve out their ways through their own efforts and to change themselves by mastering the Truth.

2

Your View of the World Changes When You Study at Happy Science

You will be able to tell whether something is heavenly or not

I imagine people who have gathered at Happy Science and studied the Truth are experiencing two major changes. One is the change in how they view the world. Before they joined us, they might have blindly followed the opinions of the general public that said, "This is valuable," "This is a great path," or "This is how you can gain the respect of others." But as they awaken to the Truth, they will develop new interests, preferences, and ways of thinking.

One example is their choice of books. They might have been casually reading books, but by learning the Truth, they will begin to see the difference between books. Among the novels they liked, some might still interest them while others no longer do. In this way, their interests and preferences will change. Which books will they lose interest in? The ones that do not contain any Truth in them. Although there are good books among works of fiction, some are mere fabrications and only seek novelty. Happy Science members will no longer find these books interesting. They will also gradually lose interest in books that only deal with three-dimensional, worldly matters. Their taste will naturally change. Whether it is literature, movies, paintings, or music, those who have learned the Truth will develop a different taste regarding what people consider "art" and wonderful. They might prefer some "art" and reject others.

Among what have been considered great works of art, some are heavenly while others are hellish. Ordinary people cannot tell the difference between them and call them all "beautiful art." But those who learn the Truth will be able to clearly see whether something is heavenly or not, be it a painting or a musical piece.

Speaking of music, true masterpieces have the taste of enlightenment, but there are also musical pieces that are filled with hellish vibrations. You will not bear to listen to them. Popular music nowadays is mostly hellish, but people cannot understand this. More people find such music great. When musicians who play this type of music hold concerts in various regions, 30,000–50,000 people flock to the venue. They are so popular that people are crushed in the crowd. It is a shame.

Yesterday, I listened to two pieces of music on records. Usually, on the day before a public lecture, I want to physically and mentally relax and ponder upon things, so I do not do anything in particular. Now, what did I listen to yesterday? One was Mozart's *Requiem*, a piece he composed before his death. It is said that the piece was left incomplete but later completed by his student. As I was listening to *Requiem*, I tried to perceive the kind of enlightenment Mozart had attained when he died at the age of 35. Then, I understood that he had attained a high level of religious awareness. His enlightenment contained sadness particular to Christianity, namely the Passion of Christ, but it was obvious he attained a very religious state of mind before he died.

The other piece of music I listened to was Beethoven's *Symphony No.9*. This piece is also known as a masterpiece and is often played in musical performances near the end of the year. As I was listening to it, I could clearly understand Beethoven's enlightenment. I understood what he grasped throughout his life. Mere music lovers cannot see this. However, those who have studied the Truth can tell what kind of enlightenment Beethoven attained and what kind of life he went through by listening to his music. They will be able to tell these things like the back of their hand. What made Beethoven suffer, and how did he get through it? What kind of enlightenment did he attain when he got through the difficulties and reached the world of delight? You will come to see these things by studying Happy Science books. It is an amazing experience.

So, whether it is music or literature, your taste will change, and you might reject some works. But you will feel great delight when you find elements that accord with the Truth in the works you have liked. Your artistic sense will develop further.

The same is true for plays. I sometimes watch Shakespearean plays. When I read them before, I thought they were kind of interesting. I liked them because they were mostly written in dialogue, and it did not take long for me to read them. But after knowing the Truth, I found deeper meaning in his plays. Shakespeare did not read the books of Truth like we are doing now, and most probably, he was not a spiritual medium. Nevertheless, he understood the Truth; the light of Truth shines in his dialogues.

Last year, I watched *Hamlet* starring Mr. Ken Watanabe. I found that many parts of the dialogue accorded with the Truth. As I listened to the words about the dead, I could see that Shakespeare had a clear understanding of the other world, or the Real World. Indeed, he did. A ghost appears in *Hamlet*, and Shakespeare's depiction and idea of a ghost show that he knew the Truth. It is obvious he knew it, including why a person would become a lost spirit.

What is more, I especially took an interest in how he described prayer in *Hamlet*. In the play, one of the main characters prays for the dead to return to heaven. He says something like, "How could my prayer reach heaven if I prayed with such a clouded mind? In fact, it wouldn't. How could he be saved if I don't correct my impure mind and attitude before I pray?" This is the principle of prayer itself. Shakespeare knew it.

Indeed, your prayers will neither reach heaven nor console the souls of the dead if you pray with a clouded mind that is full of complaints and dissatisfactions, that blames others and the environment, or that is only concerned about your desires. Shakespeare knew this. You must purify your mind before praying. As I said in "The Principle of Prayer" in December 1988 (now compiled as Chapter Five in *The Ten Principles from El Cantare Vol. II*), this is true. You can experience it for yourself and see that it is true.

Some of you might be Christians and believe you just need to follow the Bible when you pray. But if you actually communicate with the worlds of the fourth dimension and beyond, which are also known as the other world, you will obviously see how prayers reach there and what effect they have. These two points will widely vary according to the attitude of the person praying. If you pray out of selfish desires, your prayers will not truly reach the angels. Unless you correct yourself, your prayers will not reach the higher dimensions of the Spirit World. That is why you need to repent and reflect on yourself. Only with the wavelengths of a pure mind will you connect to heaven. If you pray with a "pitch-black" mind or an impure mind, you will connect to the lower, dark world.

Based on the words and expressions Shakespeare used, he clearly knew the meaning and the principles of communicating with the other-dimensional world. I do not know if he learned them from books or other people, or discovered them on his own, but it is clear he knew. This is a fact. Can scholars of English literature read Shakespeare from this perspective? I would like to ask them: After studying Shakespeare for 30 years, do they truly understand what he meant through the words his characters used?

Acquiring the perspective of the Real World

We have now successively published 60–70 books (as of the lecture). What are we publishing them for? Through these books, we are teaching how the world works and how humans should live in this world. We are also teaching how we should look at the workings of the human mind in light of the Truth—the mind that finds certain things great and certain things loathsome. People are unable to see this because no one teaches them. Schools do not teach us this. Even the religious leaders do not know this although they have inherited religious groups that were founded 2,000–3,000 years ago for tens and hundreds of generations. They do not know the truth and do not know how they should view the workings of the mind.

I am now creating "guidebooks" for you to understand the true world. That is why I am taking quite an objective, scientific, and logical approach. I have spent enough time researching and exploring things to back up my arguments and draw conclusions. During this time, I have explored the Truth from many different angles to show little by little that there is more than one aspect to the Truth. First and foremost, I want you to know what kind of world you are living in now. You will not understand this world just by being in it.

What do I mean when I say, "You will not understand this world just by being in it"? To give you an analogy, the world is just like this venue in which you are now sitting. The seats are tiered—the seats in the back are higher. The higher seats allow you to have a better view. In this world, "those in the higher seats" would mean people with higher insight and a clearer understanding of the Truth. These people sit slightly higher, so they have a clearer view. Even so, they cannot grasp the whole picture by sitting on the first floor. Sitting only 13–16 feet higher will not provide them with the whole picture.

Now, this venue has a second floor, which could be considered the other world in this analogy. Those of you sitting on the second floor are in the "other world" now [*audience laughs*]. How do you see me? I am sure you see me differently from how those on the first floor do. You are looking down on me, perhaps thinking, "Look at you. I can only see the top of your head. Why don't you look up sometimes?" Isn't that right? So, you will have a very different view just by moving to the second floor. When I speak from the podium, those on the first floor will see me like a proud teacher, whereas those on the second floor will think, "Who is that tiny guy talking?" The latter is the perspective of the Real World.

People who are dominant in this world can seem insignificant from the standpoint of the Real World. Even the haughty president of a large company would appear small in the eyes of high spirits. That is how funny he would look. The prouder he is of himself and his important position, status, or name, the sillier he would look from the "second floor." Wouldn't you agree? He would look ridiculous in the eyes of the Real World. Those on the second floor would think, "That guy is putting on airs on the podium even though he's only standing a bit higher than the people sitting there, but from the true world, he looks so small. He's far below us, and we can even see his hair whorl."

As you may have noticed, you will not be able to acquire a different perspective as long as you are sitting at the same level. Unless you change your perspective, you will not be able to see things differently. We are publishing many books so that you can acquire such an unworldly perspective while being in this world. By reading them, you can at least gain a foothold. You will surely find a foothold from which to see this three-dimensional world. When you look at other people, this world, and yourself living in this world from this foothold, you will come to see what you could not before. This is important.

3

You Can Live Apart from Attachment

How does your guardian spirit see your love affairs?

Religions often teach people to get rid of attachment. They teach you to abandon attachment or to let go of your obsession, but it is difficult to get rid of attachment no matter how hard you may try. That is because you are the one currently suffering from it. Even if you tell a man to let go of the girl he loves, he will not be able to if she is around. Even if you tell a student anticipating an entrance exam to let go of his attachment to the school he wants to attend, he might well refuse and keep studying until the exam result comes out. As you can see, a person currently suffering from attachment in this three-dimensional world often finds it difficult to get rid of it.

What if you put yourself in a completely different dimension? Suppose a man is dating his 12th girlfriend, who he thinks is the one to finally marry. He had been dumped 11 times and thinks he has a good chance of marrying his current girlfriend. Going after his 12th girlfriend and hopefully his true love, this man sees her as his last chance to get married before he turns 30 next year. If someone like him comes to me for advice, I would not be able to tell him, "Don't you think you'll have a 13th chance?" even if I wanted to, due to my position. I would just say, "I'll pray for your wish to come true."

But from a higher standpoint, this would look ridiculous. It is just another story. I want to tell him, "Many people have the same worry even at 35 or 40," but I remain silent because I cannot tell him that. Nonetheless, he is desperate because he believes this woman is his very last chance. So, he will not be able to let her go even if he is told to.

How would he look from the Real World, or the "second floor"? Believe it or not, everyone has a guardian spirit. Each person has one guardian spirit. Some guardian spirits are working hard, whereas others are slacking off and taking a nap. There are both cases, so they might not be guarding you all the time, but in principle, everyone has a guardian spirit.

How does this man—let's call him Mr. A—appear to his guardian spirit when he is fussing over his love as a matter of life and death? In most cases, there is a spiritual tie for marriage. Most people made a promise to their best partner before they were born. Now, in the eyes of Mr. A's guardian spirit, Mr. A is after the wrong woman, so his guardian spirit says, "What are you doing? She's Mr. B's wife-to-be. Why are you so desperate in going after her? She's supposed to marry Mr. B of the next division in two years." The guardian spirit wants them to quickly break up, but Mr. A clings to her with all his might. In this case, his guardian spirit has no choice but to wait for him to be dumped, which will happen. The guardian spirit prays, "Please dump him quickly."

Mr. A is after her with a pitch-black mind. In fact, he is after her not with a pitch-black mind but a lustful mind. Then, sure enough, their relationship comes to an end after six months. Having turned 30, he is shocked and disappointed. But after two years, his "savior" finally appears.

As you can see from this example, a person living in this world desperately clings onto someone. When they are put into the situation, they cannot take their mind off the person. Their mind is full of him or her. On the contrary, their guardian spirit may seriously be praying for their breakup and saying he or she is meant for someone else.

Entrance exams in the eyes of your guardian spirit

The same can be said for entrance exams. Some students are so desperate and determined to get into their choice of university that they would stake their lives on it. I knew a few people who continued to apply to medical school for 13-14 years. By the time they made it into the University of Tokyo, Faculty of Medicine, they had grown a beard and had children. Other students were surprised because they looked like professors when they were actually students. Their goal in life was to get into the University of Tokyo, Faculty of Medicine. They were over 30, so I wondered what they would do after that. But they did not think that far; they were satisfied to have entered the university that people considered most difficult.

Now, what would become of these older students? There is the medical licensing exam, and the names of people who passed it are announced every year. Although it is difficult to enter university, the results of the medical licensing exam show that the university you went to has nothing to do with your passing or failing the exam. Apparently, about 90 percent of all applicants pass it, regardless of the university they go to. I saw that about 90 percent of the graduates of the University of Tokyo, Faculty of Medicine, passed, which meant 10 percent of them failed.

The university gathers the best talent from across the nation, but that is the reality. And what if, after spending 13 years getting into the university, they fail the medical licensing exam? What will they do then? What if they fail to become doctors? That is what I would think, but the people who spend 13 years trying to get into the university do not think about it at all. They believe that getting in is all that matters. It might take them six years to graduate, only to fail the licensing exam. That would be a disaster for them; it adds insult to injury.

Their guardian spirits are thinking, "You won't make it as a doctor anyway, so you should give up now and go this way instead." But they stick to their goal and keep going to a cram school for years. They keep trying without the help of their guardian spirits. This is the reality. Such people really exist.

The importance of discovering a new perspective

As I have just explained, people in this world are given chances to make efforts on their own. You have a chance to open the way for yourself. But it is precisely because you have the freedom to do what you want that you are bound by it and believe you can do anything you want. This gives rise to attachments, which bring you suffering.

What a blessing it would be if you could adopt a different perspective at that time. What if you could look at your life afresh from a higher perspective, as if looking down from the second floor? I believe it will give you a very detached view.

Imagine how you would appear in your own eyes when you see yourself from the top of a mountain. You would probably look like an ant crawling on the ground. Then, you would wonder, "Is my suffering truly a suffering? Maybe I'm suffering only because my eyes are covered." This is by no means salvation through Other-Power. It simply means you discovered a new perspective. You found it and can now see yourself and those around you through a different perspective.

Before I entered the path of religion, I used to work at a trading company and was sent to New York as a trainee. When I returned to Japan after interacting with beautiful American women for a year, the Japanese women whom I found attractive no longer appeared that way. This may sound surprising to you, but it is indeed true. I, myself, was surprised. My attachment naturally broke off after I spent a year in the U.S. It was a strange experience.

Once I met beautiful and sophisticated women, I got used to seeing them and was no longer interested in other women, no matter how neatly they were dressed in red or yellow. I could tell at a glance whether they were elegant. Then, I no longer had any affection toward Japanese women. I am afraid that the best way to get rid of attachment is to know something better. I felt nothing from those Japanese women after that. It is strange, but you can experience such a positive effect, even in this world, if you go abroad.

4

Producing Public Happiness by Clarifying the Cause of Conflict

You will be able to recognize diverse values

Let me give you another example. By going abroad, you will be able to see your country quite well. For instance, in Japan, people are debating over how importing rice will greatly damage the Japanese agricultural industry. For Japanese locals, protecting their rice market is like God's teaching; they believe they should never import foreign rice. However, those who have lived abroad have a different perspective. I know that California rice can taste better than Japanese rice, but Japanese rice farmers who have never been abroad believe their rice is always the best. No one can change their "faith in rice." I did not have "faith in food," so I ate different kinds of rice and could tell the difference. To those of you from Akita and Yamagata Prefectures, please excuse me for saying this, but some foreign rice taste better than Japanese rice. The truth is that there are other kinds of delicious rice besides the Japanese rice that is carefully grown by Japanese farmers. Some Japanese businessmen who go to the U.S. bring back California rice in their suitcases because it is cheaper and delicious. You will only know this through experience.

If you have a different perspective, you will understand the heart of the issue. Whether you have a different perspective makes a big difference. What is the result of having a different eye or a different perspective? First, you will be able to understand other people's ideas that are different from yours. You will be able to recognize diverse values and see why and how the ideas between people in Japan and the U.S. differ and why these differences arise. Then, you will be able to make adjustments. You will be able to draw a conclusion that will balance the interests of all parties.

That is what we are aiming to achieve. In this world, people insist on various things; for example, they have different opinions on politics, economics, religion, and art. But they will not be able to reach a conclusion based on earthly judgments; their interests will only clash. But by acquiring a different perspective, you will know why people think differently, how best to balance their interests, and how you should think of their thoughts. This is an important discovery. This may not exactly be enlightenment, but you can say you have gained greater insight to live as a human being.

You will be able to see the logic in an argument

As you read my books and listen to my lectures, you will clearly understand the differences between Christianity, Buddhism, Japanese Shinto, and Confucianism. Then, with this new perspective, the argument over the separation of religion and state, for example, will sound ridiculous.

The other day, the Imperial Funeral was held at Shinjuku Gyoen National Garden. His Imperial Majesty had passed away, and the funeral was scheduled to take place, but because the state is not supposed to conduct religious activities, the ceremony was held partly by the government and partly by the imperial court. Later, scholars and others seriously discussed on TV whether the ceremony was conducted appropriately, including debates on religion. I found their arguments very funny as I watched the TV show. They did not even understand what religion is to begin with or why religion and politics must be separated. They were just insisting that they must follow the laws, which people decided on. Their discussion ran in circles—they were on different planes. It was quite funny.

One person supported the separation of religion and state by citing the former persecution of Omoto religion by the state blending with Japanese Shinto (before World War II). Then, a Diet member who studied law said that because Japanese people accepted the current Constitution that was forced on them (after World War II), they must naturally abide by it. Nevertheless, none of them understood what religion is. They said that protecting Japanese Shinto would lead to the persecution of other religions, which happened in the past. But the truth is that no matter how much they discuss this issue, they will not reach a conclusion unless they understand the position and characteristics of Japanese Shinto in relation to other religions. They did not understand the unique character of Japanese Shinto. Some even concluded that Japanese culture is a mixture of various religions. They failed to see the Truth.

Knowing the Truth means to open your eyes. It means you will be able to see the logic of the so-called intellectuals. You will clearly see the answers as to why their opinions differ and where they are mistaken. This experience will bring you joy. It is the joy of knowing, the joy of understanding the world.

Capitalism and communism
seen from the Real World

In the world of politics, too, opinions are divided into two camps: capitalism and communism. In the eyes of the capitalists, or the liberal camp, the Kremlin in the Soviet Union is generally seen as an "evil palace." People believe communists are crazy. But the communist camp, including China and the Soviet Union, disdains Japan and the U.S. as the "running dogs of liberalism." Both camps are hostile toward each other.

Then, what was the plan of the Real World? To manifest God's prosperity, many angels are born into liberal countries and are working hard in various fields, including economics, politics, and academics. They are doing their best to bring God's glory and prosperity down into this world. On the other hand, communist societies originally had the grand ideal of creating utopia. This is why communism has a religion-like power to attract people. Communism attracts so many people with its religion-like unity and activities because its goal is to create utopia. Marxist philosophy has contradictions and is out-of-date, but because Marx was passionately seeking his goal to realize utopia, there is no end to the people who are attracted to it. This is like faith. It is difficult to take this faith away from people.

As a result, a conflict of opinion occurred between them. Both sides are trying to create a wonderful world and prosperity for humanity, but a conflict occurs between them because they take different means, which makes them seem as if they are after different goals. This is sad.

What is God's true intention? Why did different opinions arise? What is the source of political and philosophical ideas? By seeking the answers to these questions, you will come to see the reason behind those differences. Even if you adhere to Marxism for 30–50 years or are a scholar of economics, politics, or the constitution in the liberal camp, you will never know the fundamental reason behind the difference in ideologies unless you study the Truth.

People only see whether something is good or evil, or orthodox or heretical, and judge it based on the outcome. They say that liberalism is right because people are more civilized and are enjoying life and that communism is wrong because people are oppressed. On the other hand, communists criticize the liberal camp by saying, "They say they are prospering and developing, but their prosperity and development are castles built on sand. They are deceived by mistaken ideologies and have become slaves to money. Don't be tempted. We must create utopia. Live righteously, even in poverty." They criticize the liberal camp as fanatic, blind believers of money, as if criticizing religion.

It is impossible to integrate these two ideas unless you introduce ideas of a higher level. It will only be a tug-of-war over power and numbers if the argument continues on the same earthly level. We must present ideas of a higher level to clearly show the reason behind different ideas. Without doing so, we will not be able to see the truth.

Many things manifest on earth and give rise to contradictions and conflicts. Happy Science aims to clarify the differences between conflicting opinions, why mistakes have occurred, and how people are inviting suffering due to their lack of understanding. This is our major goal from the macroscopic perspective or what I call "public happiness." People fight each other and create worries and suffering because they fail to grasp the correct view of the world, ideals of humanity, or righteous ideologies.

I want to make these things clear and realize public happiness. And based on a new concept, I want to create a new system and show new ways of living. Even if some ideas and ways of living do not accord with these new ways of living, I want to be tolerant toward those that embody God's Light. This is the macroscale perspective.

5

Creating Utopia in the World as You Establish Yourself

Your happiness depends on how you think

There is also a microscale perspective, although calling it "microscale" may sound rude. It may be small or large to you, but in either case, it is about matters on an individual level, about each person's mind.

Last year, I published the book *The Unhappiness Syndrome*. It has been well-received. I gave "prescriptions" to 28 types of people who are unhappy because of their worries using simple language. Many people have read the book and understood for the first time why they were unhappy. They were unhappy because of their ways of thinking. They realized that controlling their minds throughout their lives is the same as driving a car.

Please listen to me carefully. Whether you are happy or unhappy is not determined by fate. You cannot blame your guardian spirit for your unhappiness by saying it is slacking off. Your current ways of feeling, thinking, and judging make you happy or unhappy. Are you aware of this?

I sarcastically described people as suffering from the "unhappiness syndrome." Despite having the chance to be happy, they choose to do the opposite. They choose to fail and end up tormenting themselves. Why do you torment yourself so much? What is the point of doing so? You can simply turn the wheel yourself, so why don't you do it? I teach you how to control your mind because by doing so, you can solve 80 percent of your worries. You blame your environment, the people around you, your low salary, or your bad-looking spouse, but the root cause of your problem does not lie there. It lies in how you think. You may be skeptical, but if you actually control your mind, you will find for the first time that a path opens for you.

My books teach you how to control your mind. Just give it a try and see what happens. Things will truly change. You will change, and so will the people around you. Even the environment will change for the better. It is so simple. You should realize how wastefully you are living your life without knowing the power of the mind and its rules. What is more, you are dragging other people into unhappiness. The unhappiness syndrome is contagious; it will affect your family, coworkers, friends, neighbors, and others. As a result, many people will be unhappy in this world, and you will also be unhappy when you die and return to the other world. Thus, the unhappiness syndrome will spread.

This is cancer in today's society. It is the cancer of the mind, not a physical one. I have been presenting ways to cure this cancer and regain a healthy mind so that you can shape a healthy and good destiny.

My books teach you how to turn the "steering wheel" of your mind. At Happy Science, I have summarized this into the basic principle: "Exploration of Right Mind." Right Mind includes all kinds of elements. There is no end to this exploration, but why not take on the challenge?

Once you join Happy Science, you will first be required to explore Right Mind. It is not an easy thing. You must be serious and determined to explore Right Mind when you enter this gate. And once you enter it, you must keep exploring Right Mind. You must continue from the beginning to the end; you are not allowed to get off anywhere else in this journey.

I teach the Principle of Happiness or the modern Fourfold Path of Love, Wisdom, Self-Reflection, and Progress. The Fourfold Path is based on an axis called the Exploration of Right Mind. It is the first and the last, or the entrance and the exit. What is the Exploration of Right Mind? Simply put, it means to first observe how your mind works during the day. If you find the "needle" of your mind pointing in the wrong direction, or to hell, immediately turn it in the direction of heaven and God. Train yourself to do this every day. This is the condition of a Happy Science member.

You might have been aware of it when you just started out as a member but may have forgotten it after six months, a year, or two years. But that is not good. Return to the starting point and remember your resolve to explore Right Mind. Signing your name on our application means signing the contract to explore Right Mind to the end of your life. You cannot call off the contract one-sidedly. You must fulfill it. It is a contract with God. Joining Happy Science means pledging to explore Right Mind for your whole life. Then, at least one lost sheep—you, yourself—will be saved. What is more, you will neither develop an unhappiness syndrome nor spread "cancer" to others.

Happy Science values making progress based on realism

So, let us start with ourselves. Start by correcting yourself. Then, the cancer cells will stop spreading in one spot. This will work like a vaccine and affect others around you. Then, you will be able to help many people. In this way, you must first establish yourself. In the process, change other people and make the world into utopia. This is essential.

We are not mere idealists. We are also quite realistic and practical. Here is the bottom line: Did you change or improve after knowing the Truth? If not, you learned the Truth for nothing. If you have improved, you are worthy of being a member. You must check this based on the Exploration of Right Mind. The Exploration of Right Mind inevitably requires you to reflect on yourself. It also requires you to have a pure heart and to love other people. You must always purify your mind and reflect on how much you have acted for the sake of other people. This is the important point.

Happy Science values making progress based on realism and sees this as our ideal. Please do not take this lightly. Make sure to have confidence in our teachings and move forward. I am also walking on this path.

CHAPTER THREE

The Discovery of Enlightenment

The Second Public Lecture of 1989

Originally recorded in Japanese on March 19, 1989
at Kyushu Welfare Public Hall in Fukuoka, Japan
and later translated into English.

1

Finding Your Own Ground to Explore the New World

The growth of Happy Science is extraordinary; the number of members and the size of our lecture events are continuously increasing and expanding. But what I will be addressing to you now under the title, "The Discovery of Enlightenment," is certainly not about such splendor on the outside. People tend to be fascinated by big movements or momentum and forget their position, but as a seeker of the Truth, you must always come back to the starting point because what goes around comes around, and you will only reap what you sow.

Among the over 2,000 people gathered here today, I heard that over 1,000 are non-members of Happy Science. Because I cannot give a talk that only caters to our members, I will be talking about where the entrance to enlightenment is, how we can enter it, as well as how enlightenment develops. I will also talk about the state of enlightenment and how we must strive to maintain it. I will be talking about these points in the context of everyday life.

You have probably come here today because you have read at least one of my books and come to know Happy Science. I do not know which book you read first, but I am sure you have read one. What did you feel after reading it? I sometimes wonder about this and feel happy that each person has had a unique opportunity to encounter the Truth.

As for myself, before graduating from university, I had a strong desire to become a philosopher, and I was immersed in numerous philosophical and religious books. As I read through those books, I strongly sensed that something was about to happen to me. I was not exactly sure what it was, but I sensed that some sort of new mission would soon start for me. I had already read many books until then, but I had never experienced something so hot welling up inside me. It was a completely different sensation from what I would get from reading literature; I felt my soul move and shake.

I had always recognized myself as a being with a physical body, and at that time, I felt another "self" that surely existed within me. Something was shaking inside me. The other "me" started to act as if to tell me, "Now is the time to know your true self." It was a passionate feeling.

Back then, however, there was not enough material for me to judge which path I was being guided toward. So I used all the intellect and reason I had at the time to clarify what it was. I thought, "Why is such a phenomenon happening to me? What will be the consequence of all this? How should I understand what is happening to me? How will other people see this phenomenon? If 'other people' sounds vague, how will this phenomenon be judged in the commonly accepted standards of humanity?" I kept thinking about these things and focused on observing myself objectively. I think I took a sound approach regarding this point.

Why did I start by looking at myself objectively? I think it had much to do with how I had lived until the age of 24, when I started experiencing spiritual phenomena. It is true that I was seeking the Truth at the time, although only intellectually. I was reading various philosophical books, and I was reading lots of other kinds of books to cultivate myself. Indeed, I was searching for "something." I did not know what that "something" was, but I was accumulating knowledge in search of that. This is a fact.

Then, I sensed that what had been accumulating inside me was demanding I confirm this new phenomenon that was occurring. It said, "Considering the many books you have read or the philosophies of great historical figures, what exactly is happening around you? What is this voice, or this idea, trying to tell you? You must understand what it is."

When I deeply think about it now, I had no choice but to begin by relying on the piece of wisdom I had at the time to judge the phenomenon I was experiencing. Although it was not vast, I used all the wisdom I had accumulated over a short span of 20-plus years. I had a hunch that I was stepping into an unknown territory. I was about to set out into an unknown world or uncharted waters, but I had no navigator. No one knew about this ocean. I had to study this map myself and observe the sun and the stars to try to move forward. That was how I felt.

What was important at that point in time? It was that I had confidence at my core. Having experienced spiritual phenomena, I certainly had worries about how things would turn out for me. Looking back at my past, I had certainly experienced many trials and errors; there were also times when I hurt others or was unsure which path to take. Nevertheless, I could not deny the fact that I had lived single-mindedly, seriously, and earnestly. I had confidence in how I had lived and felt that this confidence would provide me with the standard to judge this new situation and the experience that I would go through in this new world.

At the time, I did not know what God or Buddha was thinking or planning for me. I had certainly made some mistakes and failed at times in the past, but if these things were removed, and if Something Absolute—God or Buddha that I had never met—exists, I thought He would surely approve of how earnestly I had been living; He would approve of how true I was to myself and my thoughts. So I thought, "This part of me should serve as a ground to explore the new world. This must be the starting point that I must always return to. In the face of a new situation, what is the unshakable part of me? What is the one thing about me I can be confident about? I will grasp this. I will make this a guide. I will make this a fulcrum of a lever, or the North Star." Without anyone teaching me, I continued to think about it and eventually found the answers on my own.

2

Starting by Discovering the "Inner Pearl" within You

There is a "core" in your mind that you can be confident of

From now on, many things will happen to you as well. You will experience all kinds of things. And as you listen to other people's opinions and experiences, you may sometimes lose sight of yourself. At that time, however, look calmly into your mind. Reflect on your past—I want to tell you this first.

There is definitely "something"—a core—in your mind that you can be confident of. This "something" may differ from person to person, but a diamond-like core definitely exists in each and every one of you. Maybe the word "exist" is inaccurate. During the decades you have lived since birth, you must have surely created something that sheds light, like a pearl in an oyster shell. You need to discover this pearl within you. You definitely have this pearl.

What is it that makes a pearl a pearl? It lies in the fact that no one can deny the value or beauty of a pearl when looking at it. This is a negative way to put it, but positively speaking, most people will see the value of the pearl. We do not have enough words to express the beauty of the pearl's brilliance. Can you describe the color and the brilliance of a pearl? I cannot; no words can describe that mystical rainbow color and brilliance. Nevertheless, everyone finds it beautiful and brilliant when looking at a pearl.

What I mean is this: Even oysters can create a pearl, so you, too, must have created your own pearl during the 20, 30, 40, or 50 years of your life. Please know this and grasp it. When you leave this world, your thoughts, deeds, and whole life will be examined, and you will have to reflect on them. At that time, will you have something you can be confident in? Please check it for yourself. You definitely have something. Knowing this "something" is the starting point for you to set out in the untrodden world and take to sea without any map or sign.

Merely accepting, memorizing, or interpreting what is written in books will not lead you to attain enlightenment. To discover enlightenment, you must first discover the "core" that lies within your own mind. This is something unique to you. It is not anyone else's but your own. You definitely have your own unique "core" you have created within you. It may be difficult for others to describe it, but you should all have a part of yourself that you are confident God would approve of if He exists. Please find out what that is for you.

This will serve as the ground to judge your thoughts and deeds from now on. Please discover the part of you that you can confidently show or talk about to others—the only thing you can confidently reveal to others. Unless you know this, no matter how much you read my books or listen to my lectures, they are just someone else's stories for you and not yours. Even if you read my books, what is written in them will not immediately become your enlightenment. The content of my books will be useful to polish the pearl within you, and it will serve as a nutrient to make the pearl bigger, but the pearl, itself, is something you must work to create on your own.

Everything starts from the discovery of the pearl within you. Discover this pearl, polish it, and develop it. In this process, enlightenment will be found. This is the first point I want to make clear today. You can think about it now or after this lecture. Or you can take time to think about it when you get home. Make sure you grasp the pearl-like core within you. Please firmly grasp the part within you that you can confidently show others without hesitation. As you explore it, you will begin to understand what kind of soul you are.

Everyone has a soul. Actually, it is wrong to say you have a soul—you, yourself, are a soul. The truth is, "The soul has a physical body." This soul has a certain disposition or a tendency. Your soul was not created and left as it was; you have also created your own disposition through hundreds, thousands, or tens of thousands of years of reincarnations. You have accumulated something, and it is deeply engraved in your soul.

The knowledge and experience you have accumulated through reincarnations—or, to be more direct, the enlightenment you have attained—is your own. No one can take it away from you. Just like how you cannot take away the color and brilliance of a pearl, you cannot be deprived of the brilliance of enlightenment you have gained through numerous reincarnations. Each one of you definitely has such brilliance.

Examining the tendency or disposition of your soul

I just used the word "reincarnation." There are perhaps more people who cannot accept this idea. But it has been eight years since I first experienced spiritual phenomena. During that time, I published nearly 70 books (as of the lecture), about half of which are spiritual messages, as you may know. It would be impossible to write them if they were a fraud or a fabrication. No one can write this much. I can do this because they are real. The world of the spirits is real.

Some may believe that people living on earth in a physical body, like you are, will become mere ash, water, and carbon dioxide after they die. They may believe that what they learned and experienced throughout their lives will come to naught. But to me, this is a fanatic and blind belief. I cannot believe such an idea. Can you? If this were true, why have you lived so earnestly and made efforts? If you end up as ashes, what are your efforts for? Why do we have morals? What is the point of having various teachings? What is the purpose of educating your children? It is nonsense if you think about it.

You feel you have to make efforts in your life because you know deep down that there is something eternal. Somewhere in your mind, you feel you must keep on improving because you know that life does not end after this one, after several decades. Somewhere in your mind, you know there is a point in making efforts because you are living an eternal life.

The memories of your past reincarnations are not something that is brought back to you by other people. In fact, you, yourself, can open the door to your subconsciousness and recall those memories. It is easy to do so. As I said earlier, one of the ways to remember your past reincarnations is to examine the tendency or disposition of your soul. What kind of soul are you? It is important to know this. This is the first step. In other words, what kind of person are you? Look back at the kind of person you have been. You are obviously different from others and have a unique character. You have a distinct character or a unique characteristic that cannot be removed no matter what.

Some people have a boundless passion for beauty. They have an unceasing zeal for what is beautiful. Artists are like this, and such people exist among non-artists as well.

Some people cannot contain their passion for beauty. That is because they clearly have this tendency in their souls. Without a doubt, they have accumulated many beauty-related experiences throughout their reincarnations. Others have a passion for studying. Such souls have undoubtedly studied many things as they went through reincarnations. They have such a tendency of the soul. There are others who are highly sensitive to music and have a unique musical sense that others do not have. These souls definitely have a history of loving music.

The tendency of your soul lies in what you are fond of the most or what you desire the most. To put it another way, it lies in something you naturally want to do when you are most relaxed. First, I want you to know what kind of person you are.

3

Knowing More about Yourself by Observing Others

Enlightenment will ultimately lead you to transcend the boundary between you and others. But at the starting point, knowing the difference between you and others is essential.

You may sometimes wonder why there are so many people in this world. There are 120 million people in Japan and five billion people worldwide (as of the lecture). They all have different faces, heights, ways of thinking, and languages. Why are there so many? Why do we need this many people? Why does everyone you meet have different ideas from yours? You may sometimes wonder about this.

In fact, other people do not just exist. They exist to teach you who you are. You will come to know yourself by looking at others. If you were born on an uninhabited island and lived alone like Robinson Crusoe, how would you know that you are a human being? You will not be able to recognize yourself. In this sense, we should, of course, be grateful that animals and plants exist. Because animals exist, you can see that humans and animals are different and understand what humans are. Thanks to other people's existence, you will know who you are for the first time. This is essential. Knowing yourself is important.

Come to think of it, animals cannot recognize themselves. Being able to know who you are is what makes human beings human. Knowing the difference between you and others and then recognizing yourself is an essential first step to enlightenment. Human beings are different from animals in that they have the ability to tell the difference between themselves and others. We have the ability to use others as a mirror to recognize ourselves.

You may have a pet dog, for example. When you show the dog a mirror for the first time, he cannot recognize that it is him reflected in it. He will probably keep barking at the mirror. After all, he has never seen his own figure, so he does not understand. He can only recognize it as an unknown creature. He cannot understand and recognize that it is himself. So dogs and other animals do not yet know themselves in the truest sense.

But fortunately, humans are given infinite opportunities to learn about themselves and others. One of the ways to learn about yourself and others is to encounter other people, like today; over 2,000 people have gathered at this venue. What do encounters bring us? Experience. We gain experience. The other thing you gain through encountering people is knowledge. We can acquire the ability to recognize things by gaining knowledge. Experience and knowledge are, in fact, the two critical sources to knowing yourself and others.

So first, as I mentioned earlier, you need to look within your mind and discover the core part—the pearl. Then, the next step is to analyze this pearl. How does your unique pearl shine differently from other pearls? How big is your pearl, and what shape does it have? You need to explore these points. You cannot see your pearl's true shape, meaning, or value by only looking at your pearl. You need to look at other people's pearls to understand your own. Therefore, the second step to enlightenment is learning from others.

Some people may believe they can attain enlightenment on their own by isolating themselves in the mountains or in their houses. But these people will end up becoming self-styled practitioners, and their enlightenment will only satisfy themselves. True enlightenment must be reliable and, therefore, verifiable. For your enlightenment to be verifiable, you must clearly know the difference between you and others. You need to know who you are in contrast to others. You need to know your own unique pearl.

So I tell you: Those who cannot see or understand others cannot understand themselves either. That is my point. You may think it is enough to know yourself by shutting yourself away from others, but your mind is already blind when you believe you know yourself. Enlightenment is not something you can attain on your own. By observing other people and examining their thoughts and the state of their minds, you must learn why human beings were created, how they are made, and what role you should play within that framework. Unless you understand this, you cannot claim to have known yourself.

Listen well. If you do not know this truth, you are no different from mere ants haphazardly crawling on the ground. In the summertime, you may have seen hard-working ants crawling on the ground. Looking at them from above, you will see how ants move forward without much of a plan. They go this way or that way while bumping into stones. Sadly, they can only react to what is in front of them. This means they can only feel, think, and act upon the situation they face at the moment. They do not learn from others before taking action. That is how they are. They do not even know where they are, where they are heading, or what obstacles they might face. They do not know these things; they only know what is in front of them.

I have to say, those who believe they should attain enlightenment alone in their own framework are like these ants. From the perspective of someone viewing things from a higher position, these people are pitiful. This example of ants shows how miserable it is not to be able to recognize oneself objectively or learn from others.

4

Understanding Others and Giving Love

Then, the next step to attaining great enlightenment is to acquire a higher perspective or greater insight. You can acquire such insight through the presence of other people and by the wisdom you gain from them. You can learn about yourself thanks to other people existing and gain knowledge by interacting with them.

To truly know yourself, first, please take an interest in other people. Some may believe they can attain enlightenment by shutting themselves away, but unfortunately, that is not the main road. Without taking an interest in other people, enlightenment is not possible; you cannot walk the road to enlightenment. Why is that? As I always teach, the true road to enlightenment is on the path from Hinayana (Small Vehicle) to Mahayana (Great Vehicle)—from establishing yourself to giving love to others. This process is the main road to enlightenment. To walk this main road, you must always take an interest in other human beings. And what I mean by taking an interest in others is not to be a bystander.

Listen well: You must not be a mere bystander. You must not be a mere critic. The interest you take in others must lead you to reflect on yourself. You must look at other people and their actions and thoughts to use them as material to reflect on yourself rather than simply become critical or judgmental. Here lies the principle of self-improvement.

What will happen as you continue this process? Your effort to improve yourself will, at the same time, work to make the world a better place. The more you improve yourself, the better you will see others. You will come to understand why people act or think in a certain way and why they face certain consequences. Being able to understand this is very important.

You may think love and wisdom are two separate things, but they are not actually separate. You cannot truly give love to other people without understanding them. You may believe you are giving love, or your actions may appear to be love, but true love must nurture others. True love must make others better.

Then, how can you tell if your love is improving others? To know that, you need to know the basics. What do I mean by the basics? Knowing the basics means the study of human beings or the general interest in human beings. Without this general study of human beings, you cannot truly give love to others; your love can end up being hypocrisy or self-deception.

For example, you may have a sense of guilt. Many of you—hundreds or over 1,000 of you here—probably have it. You may have a memory of having sinned at some point in life. You may feel bad about a mistake you made and still feel like you have to atone for it. To be free of this guilt, people do what appears to be an act of love. Some people make donations, do voluntary work, or start charitable work after retirement. But among them are many who do so out of their sense of guilt. They are doing so because *they* want to be saved and not because they want to save others. They themselves want to be free of their burden. I believe that is their motive.

Then, you will come to see there are two types of people among those who are seemingly acting out of love. One is those who appear to be helping others but are actually doing so for their own sake. Many people are like this. What is the other type of people? They are the ones who help others out of the pure intention to do so. They act because they truly want to help. They are kind because they want to be kind. Their actions and words come out naturally. In a way, they may seem too kind, but they love others because they like to love others or think it is their vocation to love others. Such people exist, too, but there are not so many of them. Those people are still very few in number.

What will be the consequences of these two types of people? What will become of people who love others for their own sake and people who love others for the sake of others? In fact, they will have completely opposite results. Those who live while loving others for the sake of others will find that they have truly improved themselves. What does this mean? Can you understand what this means? Those who help others to save themselves are only concerned about themselves. That is what they are truly thinking. They crave praise from others to console their minds. Then, what about those who always want to give love to others? What kind of beings are they? In fact, they are very much like the sun. They are becoming like the Being that keeps on giving without expecting any return. If such a Being exists in the invisible world, it must be the Will of God. The one who constantly gives without expecting anything in return is God or a being very close to God.

Being able to limitlessly give to others is a very important quality. This act brings joy. In fact, being able to give, itself, is a joy. This is the joy of a higher level. Once you truly know this level of joy, you will feel less joy in worldly pleasures or sensual pleasures. These things will no longer satisfy your mind.

Within your limited time of 24 hours a day or several decades of life, how many people can you give love to? If "giving love" sounds too vague, how many people can you nurture? To how many people can you give dreams and reasons to live for? Can you make them feel happy to be alive? Can you make someone feel blessed for being given life in this lifetime? This is what giving love means.

5

Becoming a Black Belt Holder of the Mind

By giving love, you can eliminate the hell next to you

Let me explain this further. You have probably learned about heaven and hell by reading my books, and you probably imagine that they start the moment you leave this world. However, heaven and hell are not of the other world but exist in this world. They are merely an extension of this world.

Over 2,000 people are here today, and each of you is creating either heaven or hell in your mind right now. You are sharing the same space and are sitting next to each other, but some are creating heaven while others are creating hell. You, yourself, may not know which world you are creating, and perhaps it is better not to know it. It is fine that you do not know, but you are clearly creating one or the other. This is very obvious. It is just like how a balance scale rarely keeps an even balance; one side is always heavier. In the same way, it is clear whether your life is heavenly or hellish.

Earlier, I talked about giving love. Suppose you have successfully made others feel happy to be alive or given them hopes, ideals, or reasons to live for. What does this mean? It means that although these people were sinking toward hell because of the weight, you managed to remove this weight. You have helped other people's minds ascend to heaven. In other words, at that moment, one hell has disappeared. Listen carefully. You can eliminate the hell next to you while you are still alive. It is possible to do this. I call this act "giving love."

People are sinking because of the weight; they are sinking to a level below average. They cannot take away the weight on their own because it is too heavy. They want to remove it somehow, but they cannot. The majority of people are like this. You can remove the weight for them only when you have understood them—their thoughts and ideas. What are they worrying about? What are they struggling with? How should you approach them to take the weight off their minds or alleviate their anxiety? You need to understand these things to be able to remove their weight. Remove the weights from more people and make their minds lighter. If you are able to do this, you are actually becoming an expert of life.

The ability to make people happy

If the mind is the only thing you can take with you when you leave this world, what other goal is there in life than to become a "highly ranked" expert of the mind? This is my point.

How many people's minds did you manage to alleviate? Everyone has this ability at his or her own level. You could use the term "the Black Belt of the Mind" to explain this. You may not be fully aware of this yet, but from the perspective of God, people have different levels of this ability—black belt, first dan, second, third, fourth, fifth, and so on. Some people have a higher ability and unconsciously do the work of alleviating people's minds as they interact with others every day.

In companies, people have different jobs, and some may be in charge of sales. Highly competent salespersons can produce good results every year. For some reason, they can do so consistently. Incompetent salespersons can only achieve poor results. The same goes for baseball players. Only a very few of them have a batting average of .300. Even if they temporarily fall into a slump, they always maintain a batting average of .300 by the end of the season. They have such an ability. In the world of the mind, too, there are people with a .200, .300, or .400 batting average. Increasing this "batting average" means raising the level of one's enlightenment.

Let me use this analogy of baseball to explain the meaning of self-establishment in the world of enlightenment. Players train themselves hard; they practice their swings and study different types of pitches and the pitchers of their opponent team. Acquiring the skill to maintain a high batting average through training is self-establishment for them. As a result of such training, they will become capable of achieving good results and getting a hit or home run at the most crucial moments. Then, what will happen? The spectators will enjoy watching the games, and the team members will be happy. Good players will make the games interesting and create many fans.

In a sense, the purpose of baseball lies in giving many people relaxation, joy, and enjoyment; this is the nature of baseball. Good players can practice altruism in the world of baseball. Self-establishment leads to altruism at the same time.

In addition to hitting, players can improve their pitching skills. Some pitchers can win 15–20 games a season. But will the game be dull if the opposing team is unable to hit the ball? No, it will not. The spectators will be excited to see the ultra-fast pitching, and they will admire such a pitcher. Whether you are a batter or a fielder, if you are talented, you can achieve good results and fascinate and captivate lots of people.

I used baseball as an example, but similar "games" are going on in the world of the mind every day in our workplace, family, or community. And what are needed there now are strong third batters, cleanup hitters, and ace pitchers. We also need catchers with a strong arm, excellent first and third basemen, quick outfielders, and good base stealers. We want all these good players. To make many people happy, there must be many "good players" within the world of the mind as well.

But the definition of a "good player" is a little difficult. In Japanese baseball, there is the Golden Players Club; it certifies players who hit over 2,000 hits or who threw over 200 winning games in their careers. Players with different abilities are measured according to certain criteria and are certified to join. Everyone has different characteristics, personalities, abilities, and intellectual and physical strengths. But regardless of these differences, certain criteria must be met to be a good player. What are the criteria of a good player? Be it batters, pitchers, or pinch runners, these players have performed well, brought joy and excitement to the spectators, and made the game fun. They have to be such reputable players.

Now, how can this example be applied to our ordinary lives? For example, one criterion is how your presence affects your workplace. If you have brightened up the workplace or made work more exciting, that is good. If you have improved work efficiency and made everyone happy, that is good. Or if you have contributed to improving company performance, that is also good. There are many ways to become a "good player," but at the very least, you have to understand your position first. Are you a catcher, first, second, or third baseman, or a good batter? Be aware of your position first, and then do your best. Focus on giving an excellent performance. That is important.

Improving the world and lighting up people's minds

Do you understand what I am trying to say? Let me summarize my points.

First, I talked about how enlightenment starts from discovering your own "core." You must start by discovering the "core" shining in your mind. But do not be satisfied with just finding your inner light or the "pearl" within. Next, you have to know other people. It is important to know various people and then to reexamine yourself. Through this process, you will be able to understand others and take wonderful actions, which is giving love to others. And there is yet another step. What is the next step? It is to enter the world of the experts of the mind or a way to become a "professional." You can acquire the ability to make the world better and brighten up people's minds.

So, the journey that started from taking an interest in yourself and finding the core within will lead you to turn to others and take an interest in them. Then you will once again focus on yourself and go on to explore the world of humans.

After having established yourself and recognized the outside world, you will naturally enter the path to more concretely change the world and make people more positive and better. At that time, you will need professional skills. You should not just remain an "amateur baseball player." If you are to play, do it well. Aim to be the "third batter," "cleanup batter," or "ace pitcher." There is winning or losing in baseball but not in the world of the mind. The more everyone strives, the better the world will become.

If there is such a thing as losing, it would mean falling to hell. In fact, hell was not part of God's plan, nor is it something welcomed, as you may all know. Those with mistaken thoughts temporarily go to the world of hell. In a way, they are sick people, and they have been suffering in hell for decades or hundreds of years. Some of them cannot bear the suffering of hell and escape by coming onto the earth. They possess people who are living on earth and bring them misfortune by doing bad things. This is the reality. I do not want to call them "enemies," but they could be described as such. If we were to think of them as hypothetical opponents, we could say that we are now fighting in a game to decrease the area of hell by defending and attacking well and earning points.

6

Positive Self-Reflection that Accelerates the Building of Utopia

A dangerous period that an expert of the mind will face

I just mentioned hell and the spirits in hell. I want you to think about these matters as well. This is by no means someone else's problem.

To be blunt, I could draw a line to divide the 2,500 people here to see who would go to hell: I could draw a line here (pointing to one-third of the venue) or perhaps there (pointing to half of the venue). According to the current "batting average," about half of the people would go to hell. So this is not someone else's business. You could well be one of them, don't you think so? It does not matter whether you are one of our volunteers wearing a staff armband. I cannot exactly say because I am not judging each individual. Even if you are Happy Science staff filming today's lecture, you never know. You will not know which world you will go to. So this is by no means someone else's problem. It is your own issue. You may loathe evil spirits or feel you must save them, but you yourself can become like them. What will you do then? You must consider this.

As you become an expert of the mind or an expert of life and become able to guide many people, you will experience an evil temptation, so you need to be careful. You might think, "I've completed my discipline. So now, I must point out others' bad points and correct them. There's no problem with me; I won't make mistakes anymore." Sometimes you may come to feel this way. Once you reach a certain level, you will step into a dangerous situation. You will start to feel that you are not like all the others. The same thing can happen in the world of professionals as well. This is the difficult part.

Just as it is difficult even for great pitchers to keep winning or how any good player hits a slump, you will face a dangerous period. The more you gain positive results in solving others' problems or experience extraordinary miracles and phenomena and start attracting others' admiration, the more cautious you must be.

As I mentioned in the beginning, you need to remind yourself that you, too, are just another person. If you forget this perspective, you will make a serious mistake. You may believe you are ascending on a high-rise elevator but may actually be heading downward without realizing, not knowing when or who pressed the button to the basement. You could be waiting to reach heaven, only to end up in a dark place. This can happen, so you must be careful. There are many such people. Many high-ranking people end up this way, whether or not they know about the world of the mind. Those in higher positions who have guided many people have never imagined they would be one of them. But this unpreparedness is the most dangerous.

Some politicians today are currently causing many problems (over insider trading). I do not know where they will end up until they actually die. They might be one of those who are unprepared, but they are indeed in a dangerous zone. When problems happen on a national level, the people responsible for them are tested to see how they will tackle and overcome the problems. Even a successful person is tested; when he faces an evil temptation, how will he overcome it? If he fails, he will end up in hell—that is all. If he manages to overcome it, he will develop an even higher ability to do greater work.

The same can be said for those undergoing spiritual discipline. When you acquire a certain level of ability, you will next face this kind of danger.

Mastering the Eightfold Path

Then what should you do? At such times, I want you to reconsider the meaning of self-reflection.

There is self-reflection to discover the pearl within, which you practice at an early stage. There is also self-reflection on your relationships with other people. To pursue further, there is a grander, more positive self-reflection. It is a little demanding, but you will consider whether you could have saved or nurtured more people.

The first self-reflection is to discover the Light within; the second is to examine your relationships with others. These are passive approaches to see if you have any negative aspects. In the next stage, in which you nurture others, you must start practicing positive self-reflection and consider if you have made any mistakes in *not* doing anything.

You will first focus on "negative self-reflection" and check if there are any mistakes in what you did, said, and thought. But when you enter the next stage, you need to start "positive self-reflection" and ask yourself, "Did I really do enough when I had the opportunity? Did I give enough thought or advice when I could have? I had the chance to do more, so what could I have done? Were there any other ways I could have tried?" You must do such positive self-reflection to accelerate the building of utopia. This level is quite high. Upon reaching this level, you will once again need to polish yourself further.

I will soon publish the book *The True Eightfold Path*. It comprises the four lectures on self-reflection I gave in a dojo in Tokyo. You need to be proactively giving love to others to be able to truly practice the Eightfold Path. You need the experience of giving love. A beginner of the Truth cannot truly practice the Eightfold Path.

In fact, you need to master the Eightfold Path if you want to advance from what we call "the world of arhats"—the upper realm of the sixth dimension—to the world of bodhisattvas. Without mastering the Eightfold Path, you cannot advance to a higher level on the main road to enlightenment; the practice of the Eightfold Path is indispensable.

The Eightfold Path has different elements. You need to examine yourself with the eyes of an expert.

The first is Right View. Did you see things rightly? This is very difficult. To know what is right, first, you need to discover your inner Light, gain the ability to see others, and make efforts to proactively turn this world into utopia. Only through these dynamic experiences can you see what is right. You cannot see what is right if you are confined within your own shell. By accumulating real experiences, you will come to know the world, yourself, and others, and you will see what is right. Seeing things rightly is not easy if you do not have such real experiences.

The same can be said of speaking rightly. If you cannot speak rightly, should you just sit in meditation without saying a word? No, you should not. Right speech has a positive aspect; it has the power to change the world. Words are one of the powers you can use to make the people you meet happy and to give them love. The collapse of a family or the discord and troubles in a family are all caused by words; most causes lie in words. Families fall apart due to the misuse of words.

If so, the opposite is also possible. You can build a wonderful family using words; this is definitely possible. It is very simple to reflect on such words. If there is discord between you and your spouse, see how often you have treated your spouse as a wonderful person. Have you expressed words of admiration?

Imagine you are on your deathbed, and today is your last day. Look back from the time you got married. How many kind words did you say to your spouse? Reflect on it. Perhaps you have not said much. You could have offered more kind words. You could have done so every day. You could have done so every morning, afternoon, and evening. But you did not. You will come to realize this.

7

Into the Pure World of Love

Reflect on yourself imagining you will die today

The Eightfold Path starts with Right View, followed by Right Thought, Right Speech, Right Living, and so on, and you explore righteousness in various ways. But let me put it simply.

Imagine today is your last day. Imagine your life ends today, and look back at how you have lived. Reflect on the relationships with the people you have met. You will die today; you will leave this world today. At that time, how will you look at yourself? How will you interact with others? If tears do not well up at that time, you are not a human being.

Listen carefully. If you look back at your life imagining you will die today and you do not shed a single tear, it means you have had an arid, desert-like life. You have lived without any strong feelings or emotions or without tears. Know that you are such a person. If you look back at your life and do not shed any tears, it shows who you are. It means no matter how high your position or income is, you still have a long way to go. You are far from being a true human. It means you have lived a desert-like, barren life. Please reflect on this once again.

Listen carefully. What is it that human beings should do? Whether you are young or old, man or woman, there are things you must do. All of you who have come here today, when you get home, quietly reflect on yourself alone. It is a simple thing to do. Imagine you will die at this moment, and look back at your past. Remember your parents, spouse, children, friends, teachers, and others, and know your own history of life. If tears do not well up at that time, you are not real. Or I would rather say you are not a human being. If tears do not fall, you are not a true human being. If you fail to see your true self in the dust and dirt of this three-dimensional world, you are not a true human. You have yet to become a human being. I dare say so.

Shedding the holy tears

If possible, please check each element of the Eightfold Path in order—Right View, Right Thought, Right Speech, Right Action, Right Living, Right Effort, Right Will, and Right Meditation. There are various checkpoints, and I have already explained all this. Please examine yourself against each checkpoint. Then you will be able to see many more things compared to when you first entered the gate of self-reflection.

At this point, remove the dust and dirt of your mind once again and correct the mistakes you made or wrong thoughts you had in the past. Only then will you be able to enter the world of bodhisattvas—the world of real love. To enter the world of love, you need to shed the holy tears called the rain of Dharma. Without being hit by the rain of Dharma, you cannot enter the world of love. Unless you remove the mistaken thoughts and feelings stuck to you, you can never enter the world of pure love.

This teaching is not just for you. The same applies to Happy Science executives and lecturers. Without reflecting on their minds, they, too, cannot continue to be a true human, nor can they become true bodhisattvas.

I, too, am walking the same path every day. It may appear as if I am proudly talking from a podium, but I have never ended a single day without reflecting on my way of life. This is true even now. I am now standing at the podium, but in the morning, before coming here, I spent time reflecting on myself in light of the Eightfold Path. You may be satisfied as long as you do not commit any wrongdoings, but for me, holding this first public lecture in front of 2,500 people in Kyushu would have been impossible on my own. When I imagine how many people have made efforts behind the scenes to make this happen, I cannot hold back my tears.

So everyone, I thank you very much for today. Let us continue to work together.

CHAPTER FOUR

Secrets of the Multidimensional Universe

The Third Public Lecture of 1989

Originally recorded in Japanese on May 28, 1989
at Kobe Port Island Hall in Hyogo, Japan
and later translated into English.

1

Starting by Knowing the Secrets of the Mind

The true nature of a human being

I have heard that nearly 4,000 people are here to listen to my lecture today. But this audience of 4,000 people is as tiny as a mustard seed compared with the number of people we are aiming to reach through our movement. Come what may, we must spread the power of the new Truth, its Light, and our passion to Japan and every corner of the world through our Happy Science movement.

Before I dive into the main topic, I would like you to know that you are expected to be fully aware of your mission and to be firmly determined to fulfill it. You must also know the weight of this responsibility. Whether the 4,000 of you can take on the role of changing the fate of the 5.2 billion people in the world (as of the lecture) will depend on the activities you will be carrying out from now on.

Over the past three years, I have published more than 70 books and given many lectures. I plan to conduct 44 lectures and seminars in the first half of this year alone. However, no matter how many books I write and how many lectures I give, I am often overwhelmed by the feeling of helplessness, as if I am trying to scoop out all the ocean water with a small spoon.

We are now exploring the grand views of the universe and presenting them to the world. To prove that these views of the universe are real and true, we need to be fully ready and develop a vast inner universe within ourselves that has the same structure as the outer universe. Time and time again, I have told you that there is a vast world or space in the mind of each one of you that a living person can never fathom. For example, in my book *The Exploration of the Mind*, I have described that the human mind has an onion-like structure. But even if you read my explanation, chances are that you only understand your mind through what you can see and touch; your perception of the mind is probably still limited to physical and materialistic aspects.

In the past, I have also talked about something like this: The essence of a human being can contract to a point and expand to infinity. It means that a human being can essentially contract to a single point, like closing your hand, and it can expand infinitely, like opening your hand. I have said that this is the true nature of a human being. Do you understand what it means? The "human being" I speak of refers to each one of you sitting before me. Can every one of you accept the idea that your essence can contract to a single point and expand as large as the universe? Can you confidently say that you understand this idea?

To understand this idea is the greatest enlightenment that a human being can attain while living on earth in this lifetime. When you realize and grasp the real meaning of this phrase, your exploration of enlightenment—the inner universe—and your exploration of the outer world— the multidimensional universe that surrounds you—will ultimately become the same thing despite pointing in completely opposite directions.

To know yourself means to know the world and God

Happy Science teaches the Exploration of Right Mind that is required of a human being. This is why we initially taught: "First, strengthen the inside, then the outside" or "From Hinayana to Mahayana." Many of you have probably understood that the "vector" of your mind points in completely different directions when you are seeking to build the inner self and when you are acknowledging and exploring the outer world. But today, I want to say that you must merge the inward-facing vector and the outward-facing vector into one. You must know that they are not two different things.

To know yourself means to know the world. To know yourself means to know God. To know God means to know the world God created. Then, everything will become clear to you.

The title of today's lecture is "Secrets of the Multidimensional Universe," but I do not intend to talk about outer space or the world that lies outside planet Earth. I want you to know the true secrets of the "small space" that you believe exists within your mind. Everything begins from there. What may feel like "microscopic work" will eventually turn into "telescopic work" and lead you to know everything.

2

Gratitude to God and Unconditional Love

Recognizing yourself as a part of God's life

Over the past two years, I have mainly spoken about the ways to attain enlightenment to become an arhat. Some key lectures were "The Principle of Enlightenment" (in *The Ten Principles from El Cantare Vol. I*) and last year's "The Principle of Self-Reflection" (in *The Ten Principles from El Cantare Vol. II*). I spoke much about the mindset needed to attain the state of arhat and to enter the world of bodhisattvas.

Today, I will be talking about the way to enter the state above—namely, the methods of spiritual discipline and the state of mind you should have to advance from a bodhisattva to a tathagata. I said in my very first public lecture that anyone can attain the arhat level. I also said that you can attain this level through your efforts in this lifetime. Moreover, I spoke about the difficulty of advancing from an arhat to a bodhisattva in *The Essence of Buddha*. Indeed, advancing from an arhat to a bodhisattva is the first and most difficult gateway for everyone who has gained a human soul and is undergoing soul training.

What is the decisive difference between an arhat, which is the first level of enlightenment, and a bodhisattva, which is the next level? The difference is whether or not you are fully convinced, in the truest sense, that you do not exist just for yourself. It may be difficult to understand this, so let me put it differently. I am not saying that souls in the worlds of bodhisattvas and above have no interest in themselves or have no intention to do something for themselves. They, too, have their own character, so even the souls of bodhisattvas carry out work that reflects their character. But the decisive difference is that they do not think of themselves or their individuality as their own. They have awakened to the fact that their lives are not theirs.

Do you understand what I mean by that? This is not a mere moral code. To truly know that your life is not yours means to genuinely feel that the "blood" flowing in you comes from God's enormous heart in a far, distant place. Unless you can truly feel this, you will never rise to the state of bodhisattva.

Some people may simply call this "a life of selfless service." But do they understand what it really means to live in selfless service of others? Do they understand true selflessness? That is what I would like to ask them. Being selfless is not merely a means of getting along with others. Being selfless does not simply mean to discard your ego. It means to be aware that you are a part of God's life. Unless you understand this, you have not grasped the real meaning of selflessness.

Have you ever thought about what it takes to get there? I have taught you that the world of bodhisattvas is basically a world of love that gives, a world of love that keeps giving, and a world of love that gives without expecting anything in return. And to understand that love is essentially an innate part of you, you need to accumulate long years of experience.

You will never understand love through knowledge or ideas alone. For love to be fully established, it must be practiced. What does that indicate? Do you understand what I mean by "love must be practiced"? It means that you, who have a name and are confined and limited by a small physical body, will have the urge to go beyond your own framework and expand yourself. The true nature of love is the self-development of each one of you, who is a child of God. It goes without saying that self-development that arises from ego is not called love. Your development turns into something wonderful only when you recognize yourself as a part of God's life and strive to develop yourself in that way. Therefore, if many of you here have already encountered the Truth, cleared the clouds over your minds, and attained the state of arhat, your goal from now on is to expand the self through the practice of love. If you are expanding and extending yourself in the truest sense, it means you are already living a sacred mission.

Breaking your shell of self-limitation

Now, I would like to talk in more detail about the love required of those at the state of bodhisattva.

Let me ask you a question. Do you know what love is? What is love? I have talked a lot about it and written many books about it. You have probably read them. Did you understand love? Love is something that brings warmth to your heart. Otherwise, it is not love. Love is not empty words. It is not something you just think about in your head. Love is not the deeds that are superficially regarded as good. As you try to make your thoughts a reality, your heart must get warmer. If not, then that is not love.

For your heart to get warmer, you need passion. What is the source of passion? It is the energy that gushes forth when you break the shell of your soul. By "shell" I mean self-limitation. It is the thought that binds you as a human with limitations—your education, environment, and beliefs that you have had since birth. It can also refer to conventional ideas. These things are binding you. When you free yourself from these shackles, break the shell, and release the infinite energy within, love will burst forth as strong passion.

Some people act while thinking, "I should do this because it is good" or "I shouldn't do this because it is bad." But if your actions only come after such speculations, they do not deserve to be called love. Love is more fundamental. It comes from a deeper part within you. It is far more powerful. It is a power that comes from a much deeper part within you.

For this power to come forth, you must know how much you are being sustained and nurtured. Those who do not appreciate this do not know love. I have said this before. If you look back at your own past and realize that you have never loved anyone, you have probably never appreciated anyone either. Moreover, you have probably never thanked everything in this world or the great God or Buddha. Gratitude and love are two sides of the same coin. By realizing how much you have been given and sustained, you will be led to realize what you must do. Only then will the love that arises from gratitude be selfless and unconditional.

To keep giving the love that accords with God's Will

You can start practicing love that gives, which I just spoke of, at any fork in the road in your life by renewing your resolve to do so. However, over time, your love can become discolored or distorted. That is why I have presented the Eightfold Path as a necessary means of correcting yourself.

I published a book titled *The True Eightfold Path*. It teaches the eternal Truth. The self-reflection guided by the Eightfold Path is by no means far from love. In order for you to keep giving the love that accords with God's Will, you need to examine and correct yourself in light of the Eightfold Path. So, the Eightfold Path is still a required practice in the second stage of spiritual training for bodhisattvas. As you practice love that gives, you must also correct yourself by practicing the Eightfold Path. Bodhisattvas still need to practice it. Then, as we practice love that gives and the Eightfold Path over and over again, we will arrive at the next truth. The continuous practice of love that gives and the Eightfold Path will lead us to the Six Paramitas.

3

Recognizing Yourself as "Work" Itself

Putting your entire life into fulfilling a sacred mission

As I explained in detail in *The Golden Laws*, the Six Paramitas are indispensable spiritual training to advance from a bodhisattva to a brahma. The Eightfold Path at the level of arhat is still focused on self-perfection, but once we get to the stage of Six Paramitas, the emphasis greatly shifts to altruism. In this stage, you are seeking the way to become more active or to make the best use of yourself for the sake of others. However, I will not go into the details of the Six Paramitas today.

What I want to teach you in today's lecture is about the state of brahma, which is the upper part of the bodhisattva level. You may have noticed that I sometimes use the word brahma in my books. What is brahma? It is explained as the level between a bodhisattva and a tathagata. According to another explanation, brahmas are actually tathagata-grade spirits who are doing bodhisattva-level work.

Those in the state of brahma express themselves in a completely different way from bodhisattvas. Those regarded as bodhisattvas carry out their activities while retaining some level of awareness as human beings or, to put it another way, having physical senses, just like you do. However, those at a higher level—or in this case, the brahma level—do not recognize themselves by their hands, legs, or face, as you may with yourselves. Unlike people living on earth, they do not recognize themselves as having a certain body and doing certain work but rather recognize themselves as their "work" itself. Do you understand what I mean?

Perhaps you, too, had the experience of being immersed in your work. When you feel your work is your calling and become absorbed in your work, you sometimes forget about yourself. But most of the time, those moments are temporary and do not last very long. This is not the case with those at the state of brahma. They are brahmas because they are aware that they are the very work they do. This means their work is what they are and nothing else. By "else" I am referring to a private, human-like life.

Brahmas no longer have private or personal lives. They are actually working 24 hours a day. What does it mean to be working 24 hours a day? It means they are putting their entire life into fulfilling a sacred mission. Try to look back and reflect on your own 24 hours and the decades past. What do you see? Look at your life in light of the Truth that you have started learning. What percentage of your day or the decades past have you spent on the Truth or lived based on the Truth? How many people can say, "I spent the majority of my life for the Truth"? This percentage may shrink the more you think about it. In fact, this low percentage indicates what level your soul is at right now.

Examine your attitude toward studying the Truth

To reach the state of brahma, you must devote all of yourself to the Truth. You must devote hundreds or thousands of years of your soul's life to the Truth and have no regrets. It is not enough to "like" your work. Your work must be accompanied by the kind of joy that moves you from the bottom of your soul.

Let me give you an example. Each person takes a different attitude when he or she reads books of Truth. A person might think that "I have to" or "I must study" and read based on a "have-to attitude," whereas another person might think, "This is indispensable nourishment for my soul." Yet another person might read the books knowing that learning the Truth is their joy, whereas a fourth person might think, "Learning will immediately lead to action." A fifth person might read them thinking, "These books tell me what I must do. Absorbing and practicing the contents is a joy for my soul." In this way, people's attitudes may differ. You can see a glimpse of the nature of your soul in your reading attitude.

It is like being able to identify fish by just looking at a single scale. You do not need to see the whole fish. You do not need to look at the barbels—a carp has carp scales, a goldfish has its own, and so does a sea bream. Your attitude toward studying the Truth instantly tells who you are. To know the nature of your soul, you just need to ask yourself using what I said as a reference.

After examining yourself, if you conclude that you still have a long way to go in your spiritual training, then turn over a new leaf today. But if you feel that a "scale" of yours is emitting a great light, what should you do? A carp has its own way of swimming, and so does a sea bream. Likewise, awaken to your own. Know what it is that you must do. This is important.

Start by learning what the glimpse of your soul is telling you. Then, in every aspect, no matter what position you are in, take a step or two forward beginning today.

Moving away from the human perspective

So far, I have explained that the brahma state lies above the bodhisattva state and that brahmas perceive themselves not by their appearance but by the work they do. Therefore, we can say that those in the brahma state and above are beyond the frame of human beings.

Once you gain the perspective "I am work itself," a great change will occur. This is quite hard to understand with an earthly perception. Here on earth, there are constraints to our work. For example, when you have a conversation, it is one-on-one. Humans do not think of other ways than to speak one-on-one. This is how humans work on earth. Of course, it is possible to speak to multiple people, but based on an earthly perception, humans on earth limit themselves and believe they can only converse with one person at a time. That is because humans only have one mouth, two eyes that only face forward, and only two ears. They believe they are meant to talk with the person in front of them.

Now, how about those in a higher dimension or, in particular, the upper part of the Bodhisattva Realm or the seventh dimension? For example, I am speaking to 4,000 people in the audience now. This can be explained as having 4,000 of me in a three-dimensional way. From an earthly point of view, there would be 4,000 Ryuho Okawas working at once. That is how those in the upper part of the seventh dimension perceive it. Do you understand what I mean by this? Each person is speaking one-on-one with me, yet there are 4,000 people I am simultaneously speaking to. Because we are in the earthly world, it appears that 4,000 people are facing me and I am facing and speaking to 4,000 people. But that is not how it is in the Real World. I can talk to these many people while each of them simultaneously feels that they are speaking one-on-one with me. Such a thing is possible because my self-recognition is no longer based on the physical body. I do not recognize myself as a human being named "Ryuho Okawa" with physical limitations. My true nature is the very work of speaking to thousands of people. That is what I am.

Do you understand this shift in awareness? If not, you will not understand the multidimensional universe, so please restart from the arhat level. To understand the teachings on the universe, this shift in awareness is necessary. But usually, people can only recognize themselves based on their physical senses.

Can you see yourself from a different perspective? For example, we are in this hall today. Can you think of yourself as being this hall? Imagine yourself to be this hall with thousands of seats; you are now accommodating thousands of people and are holding this lecture event. Can you change how you recognize yourself like this? If you can, you will be able to move away from the human perspective. It means you will be able to move away from your earthly attributes.

4

The State of "Universe as Self"

(1) Your soul ascends high above and sees Planet Earth below

In the past, I have also stated that those at the brahma state have spiritual powers of a completely different level; they have attained the avalokitesvara level and acquired the ability to see through everything. In the truest sense, this ability is acquired at the brahma level and above. I have also said that this ability will ultimately lead you to understand the great universe. To put it another way, you need to shift your recognition as a prerequisite to understanding the great universe. I talked about imagining yourself to be this hall and seeing this lecture from that perspective. What if you expanded it further? It means you can become the universe. If you expand yourself further, you can become the universe. You can become the great universe itself and see its inner world. I am referring to this possibility.

In the past, several people experienced the state of becoming one with the universe. I have spoken about this too a few times. I have taught that there are three levels to this awareness of "universe as self." The first level of "universe as self" can be attained at the level of the Sun Realm in the strict sense, which is the highest level of the Tathagata Realm. It is the level of awareness that tathagatas such as Socrates attained. Some people, including Socrates, experienced oneness with the universe. In their experiences of oneness with the universe, their souls left their physical bodies while they were still alive on earth, ascended and expanded infinitely, and saw planet Earth below them. They saw Earth as a small sphere. This was their experience of "universe as self."

The "universe as self" in the eight-dimensional Tathagata Realm is only possible based on the assumption that Earth exists. That is the limitation. Socrates experienced this. His experience of oneness with the universe is clearly described in *Phaedo*, which he had Plato write later. It is clear that Socrates experienced gazing down on Earth from far above. He clearly spoke of it.

(2) Your consciousness expands to the size of a galaxy

The higher level of oneness with the universe is the awareness of "galaxy as self," so to speak. It is a state in which your consciousness expands to the size of a galaxy. You will see Earth as a small, cell-like being.

(3) You will see the great universe as one living entity

Then, what about the third level of oneness with the universe, which is yet a higher level? In this state, you can see the great universe as one living entity. Let me put it in a way that is easier for you to imagine. Imagine yourself to be a tiny, microscopic being inside your own body. You are a virus-like being. How would you see yourself? Your body would be an enormous universe where various parts with their own functions come together.

Now, how would a galaxy appear to a person who has attained the third stage of "universe as self"? In truth, what we call a galaxy exists in astronomical numbers. The Milky Way Galaxy that we can see from Earth will look like the human heart. It clearly looks like the heart. And the group of planets in our solar system, with the Sun at its center, will look like an artery. God's Energy, or God's Light, is pumped out from the center of the universe, travels through the galaxy, which is the heart, and powerfully pours into the solar system. Through this large artery, or mainly the Sun, God's Light flows to Earth, Venus, and other planets. That is how the universe looks to someone who has reached this third stage.

Looking through a telescope, outer space looks like a gathering of small stars in empty space. But to the spiritual eye, it looks like a single living organism—a body moving with a grand mission. Suppose the universe raises its "right hand." What does it mean? It means that great changes will happen in the local star clusters; new stars are born and a new solar system is formed.

Just as illnesses sometimes disable parts of the human body, a star could also die, or a group of planets around it could wither and disappear. Black holes look like cancer cells. To the spiritual eye, they appear dark and sooty, just as cancer cells do. Like cancer cells, they suck the life out of anything that comes close to them. What is it that comes near them? They are nearby planets or the "cells" within a galaxy. Cells close to the cancer cells will be encroached upon, eaten away, and sucked in. These black holes are like cancer cells.

In this way, a highly functional body has been formed in this vast, galactic universe. Using various places as footholds, the universe carries out activities. But just as a human body develops various problems, the galactic universe also develops "sick areas" as it conducts activities despite being a huge body separated from God. And these ill-stricken areas are spots of conflict.

The main goals of our solar system

Each planetary group has a goal. A group of planets has its own goal of evolution. The solar system containing Earth has goals and ideals of its own that are different from those of other solar systems.

What are the goals of the Earth-led solar system? At this stage, it has two main goals. One is to raise intellect to infinite heights. Intellectual evolution is one of the major goals. Another goal is to achieve great harmony at the same time. This will lead to beauty. Intellect and beauty are the two goals of our solar system.

But beings in other galaxies and solar systems carry out activities with entirely different goals. Friction occurs in places where groups with such differences overlap, and these places often turn into black holes. This can be observed at the third level of oneness with the universe.

The state of "God as self"

There is yet a higher level of awareness than this third stage of "universe as self." It is "God as self." At this stage, the universe no longer looks the way it did in the third stage, where the universe looks like parts of God's body, such as the heart, organs, or blood vessels. As you raise your awareness, the universe will begin to look like a single sphere. It will look like a small ball. You will see many of these balls floating in an even greater universe.

These balls are called the thirteen-dimensional universes. From an even higher fourteen-dimensional world, these thirteen-dimensional universes truly look like balls floating in space. And as you can imagine, these balls form groups and make up the next level of order. These floating balls come together, and just like the galaxy I spoke of earlier, they form the heart, the kidney, the stomach, or the brain of an even larger universe.

Where is our universe located?

Here is a question for you. Looking at the thirteen-dimensional space ball that contains our Earth from the higher, fourteen-dimensional universe, which part of the human body do you think it corresponds to? In fact, when seen from a higher universe, the universe we live in corresponds to the eye in the human body—the right eye. That is where we are located. We are living in the "eye" of the fourteen-dimensional universe and higher. The eye is made up of cells. Each and every cell is a tiny galaxy, even though they appear vast in our own eyes. We live in such a world.

Why does our world correspond to the eye? This vast universe we live in serves as a window through which we can see the world created by God. Through this universe we live in, we can easily see all the other worlds. That is our universe. In other words, the universe we live in is a representative work among the worlds God created. Various elements of God's ideals have been collected here. Like in a miniature garden, many events that can serve as case studies or examples are happening here. That is our world.

5

Our Mission from
the Perspective of the Universe

Reading this far, you now probably understand the mission of the Earth's spirit group or the mission of the spirit group of our solar system. We are a very proud group of souls. Great things are expected of this universe, even from the perspective of a far larger universe. God has placed great expectations especially on us, who live in this solar system in this galaxy. Such is our soul group. This is true even from a larger, macro perspective.

I am not saying this just because I live on Earth. Viewed from the standpoint of an even larger universe, our soul group is quite advanced and possesses a grand ideal. A large number of these souls are living in physical bodies in this 20th-century world. Please understand the significance of this. Please know just how great a mission we are expected to carry out in this lifetime.

You are here in a physical body in the world of the 20th century and have gathered under a great calling to be part of this great movement. This is not a coincidence. The chance of you gathering here when seen from this great universe is not even one in a trillion but is one in a trillion times a

trillion times a trillion. Indeed, you are chosen souls. You
were chosen not by chance but by fate.

Now that you know this fact,
Can you stay as you are?
Can you stay asleep?
Why not wake up?
Why not take action?
Why not rise up now?
Do you really think
You can live out your life to the fullest
As you are now?
You are not a mere physical being.
We were born into this world
With such a great mission.
If so,
Imagine how much work and action are expected of us!

From now on,
Stop being a mere human being!
In this multidimensional universe,
You were born under an extremely slim chance.
Much is expected of your soul.
Imagine how much work is expected of you.
Compared to beings on other planets,

You are in an extremely advantageous,
Blessed environment.
In such an environment,
You must not live lazily!
You must not regress!
Make up your mind
And awaken to this great mission.
From now on, let us strive together.
Thank you very much.

CHAPTER FIVE

The Ultimate Self-Realization

The Fourth Public Lecture of 1989

Originally recorded in Japanese on July 8, 1989
at Sonic City Large Hall in Saitama, Japan
and later translated into English.

1

The True Nature of Self-Realization

Looking back, it was just about three years ago, around the time of the Milky Way Star Festival on July 7, that I had decided to establish Happy Science—I had a week left at the trading company before I resigned. People asked me what I was going to do after I resigned, and I told them I was going to start *Kofuku-no-Kagaku* (Happy Science). The name sounded odd to those who heard it for the first time. The words *Kofuku* (Happy) and *Kagaku* (Science) are joined using the particle *no* (of), but the name does not have a word like "association" in it and gives no indication of what it is. I remember feeling a little embarrassed when I said that name.

Nonetheless, we have continued to conduct various activities for three years since then, and now the name Happy Science, which was unfamiliar at the beginning, has been established as a proper noun. I believe the name has become firmly rooted in people's minds, like a signboard. In this way, I have witnessed something that was invisible and formless turn into something tangible through everyday activities. On seeing it, I was struck by an indescribable sensation. But I am sure I am not the only one who feels this way. An ideal that originally lay in a person's mind was spoken through his mouth, and the words spoken through his mouth were eventually accepted by many. When his words were accepted by many and called for action, the words manifested in a tangible form in this three-dimensional world.

Considering this process, I sense that it is somehow different from the so-called self-realization that is popular these days. People generally understand self-realization as the fulfillment of their worldly desires and are happy when these desires are fulfilled to a satisfactory level. But my honest feeling is that I sense a deeper and more mystical tone in the term *self-realization*—I felt some kind of great stream in that word. It is a mystical sensation that the stream is flowing from the Milky Way. From a far, distant world, it continuously flows, heading toward the Earth, until it runs across the surface of the Earth and flows off. An indescribable Great Will is at work to make it happen; it tries to manifest its power in this world with a specific direction. The word "self" in self-realization is far from sufficient to describe this process. It does not convey enough meaning. That is how I feel.

Currently, *Happy Science Monthly Magazine* runs a series called "Love Blows Like the Wind." Just as love blows like the wind and passes through one person's heart to another, passionate energy flows from a far, distant galaxy and passes through this world without people noticing its presence. For me, this is the true nature of self-realization.

Talking about self-realization, you might focus on the results. What kinds of results or outcomes have been produced? That is how many people understand self-realization. However, I do not think this is the true meaning of self-realization. When I hear the words of successful people who are known as giants of "self-realization," I feel as if they are confined in a shell. To me, they appear to be trapped inside a cocoon. Perhaps their shells are not as soft as cocoons. Sometimes, their shells look like a block of concrete. Their hearts are confined inside this hard shell. Their hearts have hardened so much that their true selves never come out. Their hearts are covered by a shell called "ego." If that is the result of self-realization, we must not make it our ideal.

Forgive me for using literary expressions to describe this, but to me, the ultimate form of self-realization is like the wind. It is infinitely pure and transparent and is boundlessly passionate; it blows through people without even hoping to be recognized. The purer and more transparent you are, the higher your level of self-realization. This is how I feel.

Almost three years have passed since I entered the world of religion. In these three years, I have published books, given lectures, and done various other things. However, if the work I do in this world only hardens my innate divine nature, as if covering it with concrete, then such work would feel very empty to me. In reality, as my work increases, more three-dimensional vibrations will come at me. Each and every one of your wishes and prayers will also come at me. The worries and sufferings of each one of you will come into me. I can sense that you are suffering from the invisible shackles in this three-dimensional world. As I make efforts to help remove these invisible shackles or yokes from people, I, too, am tainted by these three-dimensional vibrations without realizing it. Recently, I have felt sad about this consequence.

However, this is not how it should be. No matter what earthly problems may appear before me, no matter what earthly difficulties may stand in my way, my heart must not become hard like an iron lump in trying to solve those problems. If it becomes hardened, it would mean my defeat. Self-realization is not about solving earthly problems or overcoming evils using the power of this three-dimensional world. As you live in this three-dimensional world, you must embody the power of the world beyond this earthly world and keep letting it flow like the wind. You must be the wind itself and keep blowing through. Only then can you achieve the self-realization you can be satisfied with in this lifetime.

2

The Fourfold Path Is the Key to Achieving the Ultimate Self-Realization

Let me take you back to the distant past, to 4,300 years ago. There was a man named Hermes in Greece. You may have heard of his name from Greek mythology. The Greek myths have been handed down incorrectly—it is now mistakenly believed that Hermes was one of Zeus' children, but the truth is that Hermes was born in Greece several hundred years before Zeus and sowed the seeds of love and progress in the Greek lands. That was what Hermes did.

The seeds of love that Hermes sowed continued to grow through the ages. One of them appeared in Israel in a different form, as the love of Jesus. The teachings of progress Hermes gave were handed down through the ages and eventually led to the modernization and prosperity of the Western world. Hermes taught people two wondrous concepts: love and progress. Here lies the key to understanding the title of today's lecture, "The Ultimate Self-Realization."

Happy Science teaches the modern Fourfold Path or the four right paths of love, wisdom, self-reflection, and progress. Love and progress of this Fourfold Path come from Hermes' thoughts that I just mentioned. Wisdom and self-reflection come from Buddha's teachings in India. I am now trying to integrate these into one grand teaching, which has never been done before.

Love comes first in the Fourfold Path, but it is not for the sake of convenience. It necessarily comes first because it is the most important. I teach everyone, "First, have love." Many people may think the teachings of Happy Science are so vast that they have to study a lot and absorb a lot of knowledge. But take a close look at the order of the Fourfold Path. First, have love. Be a person of love. Be a person overflowing with love. This is what I am saying. The starting point of love is "love that gives." What I am asking of you at the starting line is not so difficult. Those who have come to Happy Science to find happiness may also hope to receive love in some form. However, I tell you first: "That's not the right attitude. Love begins by giving." This is what I teach.

If the other teachings are difficult for you, you may forget about them. If you have encountered the word *love*, grasped this one piece of Truth that love begins by giving, and if you can live by it throughout your life, then that is good enough. Knowing "love that gives" is the starting point of living a heavenly life as human beings in this world.

In addition, if possible, I want you to take this opportunity to learn the many teachings of the Truth. Please deepen your wisdom to train your soul, to gain a better understanding of the world, and to understand more people. Then, use the wisdom you have deepened to reflect on your thoughts and deeds. This is self-reflection. When you have corrected your mistakes and purified your mind through self-reflection, move toward progress while keeping that pure mind. Progress is a road leading to utopia. This is the order I want you to follow.

The Fourfold Path consisting of love, wisdom, self-reflection, and progress does not end after progress but leads back to love. When you are making progress, you are apt to be enamored with its splendor and become attracted to worldly success. At that time, you must stop and think: "Wait. I started from love. I started by giving love, but as I have pursued great progress in this world, I unconsciously became caught up in earning praise, reputation, and high esteem just for myself." Then, you will find that you were unknowingly taking love despite having started by giving love. That is why you must go back to the starting point: "love that gives."

Thus, you must raise your level of the Fourfold Path, little by little, as you go through its cycle. As you practice this Fourfold Path repeatedly and raise its level, you will develop yourself further as a human, and your environment will become much brighter.

3

Hermes Sought "Progress from Love"

Lighting the candle in the hearts of others

I sincerely hope that you master all four paths, of course, but today, I will focus on love and progress and talk about them in detail in connection to self-realization.

As you may have read in our monthly magazine, Hermes was a hero. However, he was different from a military hero who embodies what we call the Red Light of Justice. How was he different? He was clearly different in his starting point. Hermes started with love, and because he sought progress out of love, he was not simply a hero of justice. In the process of achieving his goal, he fought against various countries. With the goal of unifying all of Greece, he began his work at around the age of 30, and for 36 years, until he passed away at 66, he never gave up his dream of unifying the whole area. But his dream was different from the ambitions of Japanese feudal lords who simply wanted to rule the country during the Warring States period. The difference was that Hermes fought for love. It was a fight for love.

Hermes had the following philosophy at his basis: "Each and every person has an unlit candle in their mind. Everyone, including you here and you over there, has a candle in their heart that has yet to be lit. Lighting this candle is the act of love. What is the act of lighting the candle? It is to bring out the light, brightness, wealth, and strong hopes in people so that they can emit these innate qualities from within. To help them do so, you must light each person's candle. That is the important thing." Hermes thought in this way. He clearly saw the divine nature that was dormant in the mind of each person. He thought, "How can people live their lives without realizing their divine nature? Many of them are living in this way. So, if I can't even light a single candle during my life on earth, what's the point of my life?" That is why he took action and carried out heroic deeds.

Shakyamuni Buddha was meditative and reflective. He looked deeply into his mind and developed his philosophy. But Hermes was a man of action. Why? It was because he was convinced that the candle within each person would never be lit unless it was lit individually. That is what he believed. A big fire, like a forest fire, would not light those candles. It would instead burn and kill everyone holding their candle. Candles are not lit with such a big fire. Each person's heart is delicate and sensitive, so each candle must be lit with kind words, one at a time. Otherwise, you will never be able to fulfill their hopes and wishes.

Then, what happens when you have such thoughts? You will need to carry out infinite activities. What does that mean? It means you must overcome any three-dimensional obstacles to carry out your activities. Just as the wind comes from nowhere and blows through people, gently caressing each person's cheek, Hermes needed to carry out such activities. What is this gentle wind? It is felt when a person who embodies love appears before each person and teaches what love is through their very presence. This was Hermes' philosophy.

Love is like the wind

Hermes would often teach people in the following way:

You say you want to know love?
If you want to know love,
Look into my eyes.
Look at the light in my eyes.
What brilliance do my eyes possess
When they look at you?
The pure Aegean blue eyes are looking at you, aren't they?
This blue color is infinitely beautiful.
When you bathe in this blue,
You might think you, too, will be tinted with blue,
But you won't.
That's right.

Although I give you the wind named "love,"
This wind will never be yours.
Although I become a wind and visit each one of you,
You cannot capture this wind with your hand.
You cannot make it your own.
Even so, never forget this wind and how it felt.
This is the wind of love.
This is the Aegean blue.
Never forget its touch.
Never forget its beauty.
And create it on your own.
The Aegean Sea was not dyed with blue paint.
Each particle of water makes it blue
By absorbing and reflecting sunlight.
Do you understand how much of a blessing
The work of each particle brings to Greece?
Reflecting sunlight is the best each particle can do,
But what do they produce altogether?
The inexpressible blue color.
They produce the kind of blue
That cannot be found in any corner of the world.
They shine with mystical brilliance.
Remember this.
Love is the same.
Even if someone shows you love,
It will not be yours.

But you can learn from that example
And try to create the same thing yourself.
You can proactively create something similar
Through your own actions.
That's how love is born.

Look into my eyes,
For they will speak eloquently.
They will speak more than my mouth.
It is these blue eyes that will teach you.
That is how the Truth has always been.
When people look at a shining diamond,
They wish to be like it.
The work of a diamond is complete
When it displays its brilliance.
A diamond completes its work of love
By teaching each person that such brilliance exists.
Even if you try to make a diamond your own,
It will never be a part of your body,
Nor can you bring it back with you to the afterworld.
A diamond shows us love
Just by existing and continuing to shine.

All of you, listen to my voice.
I am the light of this diamond.
My light descends on earth once every few thousand years

To teach you what the true light is.

However,

None of you can take hold of this light

Or possess it.

None of you can make it your own.

But listen well.

I will continue to shine.

Never forget this brilliance.

Make sure to imprint this brilliance

In the back of your eyes.

Keep this brilliance alive

Somewhere in your memory.

I have come to show you

The brilliance of light.

Remember this brilliance.

Know this brilliance.

And strive to work hard

And find ways to make it your own

Throughout your life,

For decades,

For centuries,

For millennia to come.

Hermes often spoke like this. Please think deeply about the meaning of these words.

Love...
People say they can receive love from others,
But simply receiving love does not make it real.
For love to be real,
You must reflect light
Like the water particles of the Aegean Sea.
It means that
If you have received love,
You must know what it is.
Knowing love means
Knowing that to love is to give.
Once you know that to love means to give,
What will you do?
You will surely start taking action
To pass on the goodwill you received to others.
That is how love is.

Love is light
And the "chain reaction" of light.
No one is allowed to keep it for themselves completely.
As long as the light continues to work without stopping,
It will stay on earth as unceasing brilliance.
But the moment love stops its work,
Light will also cease to shine.
That is love.

Light manifests through actions.
Light manifests through continuous actions.
When light stops producing a chain reaction,
The light of love dies.
Then,
Love will cease to exist.
Just as wind is no longer wind
When it stops blowing,
Love is no longer love
When it stops being passed on from one person to another.
Then,
Love dies.

I am certain you understand these words. To love is to give, but even if you give love to someone, he or she cannot keep it forever like they would an object. Love grows and expands by continually being given; it gains life as it circulates among people. It is like the wind. It is like the flowing river. If it is cut off, the river is no longer a river. A river is what it is because it flows continuously without stopping. That is the true nature of a river. Love is like the wind and also like the flowing river. I can say so.

4

Seeking the Infinitely Selfless Heart

Now, let me ask you: What does it mean to know love? What does it mean to have understood the teachings of love? You should be able to answer these questions after hearing my explanation. Even if you were able to give love to someone today, your love might stop the moment you give it to them. Or perhaps it will not stop there and instead be passed on to the next person and then to another. Did the seeds of love you sowed wither and die, or did they bear abundant fruits? How would you know? You may see the results by learning how the person you gave love to turned out to be. But let me tell you one thing. The proof as to whether or not the seeds of love you sowed firmly took root lies in your own mind. It does not lie in the reactions of others. To confirm that your seeds of love landed on fertile soil, you must see some kind of reaction within you. Please know how beautifully you will shine by giving love. That is what is important. If you are giving love out of pretense, your mind will not continue to shine beautifully. For your seeds of love to truly take root and bear fruits, you, who have given love, must keep shining beautifully.

What is it that prevents you from continuing to shine beautifully? What do you think hinders your beauty? Let me give you a hint. The hindrance to your beauty is your memory of having given love to someone. It is your attitude of taking pride in your actions. It is your sense of self-satisfaction that you did something for someone. Yes, such thoughts are blocking the light of your soul.

You probably understand why I say, "Blow like the wind." The wind does not let people know it is there. It does not show itself, but it surely exists and strokes our cheeks. Yet, we cannot see or catch it. This is what I mean when I say, "You will shine ever more brilliantly by making your mind infinitely pure and clear like the wind." Yes, it is a noble act to give love. But counting, listing, and remembering how much you have given to others is the same as dying the wind with color; the wind will no longer be pure. If the sand named "self-assertiveness" is mixed in your wind, it will blow fiercely like a spring storm, blowing a gust of sandy wind onto people and hurting their eyes. If the desire to show off or if selfishness gets mixed in your wind called "love," it will become like a tornado that carries sand and gusts of wind. You must not let sand or dust get into the wind. Remove the sand or dust. Do not have such egotistic thoughts.

In the course of your life, how many times have you thanked the pleasant, fragrant breeze? Once? Twice? Three times? Perhaps never? The answer varies from person to person. Nonetheless, regardless of whether or not you feel grateful for the wind, it continues to blow and reminds you of the feeling each season brings. The wind keeps on blowing to give us a clear, crisp, and refreshing feeling. Yes, indeed; think of the wind as your ideal image of love. Be an ideal wind. Do not hurt others or blow too strongly. And do not stop blowing. Like the wind, pass on love from person to person without picking up sand.

Happy Science is now in its third year of activities and is undergoing change. We are in a transitional period and are trying to move onto the next phase. In the last three years, we focused on exploring and learning the Truth. I believe we achieved success to a certain level so far. But from now on, we will be entering the age of missionary work. And when you convey the Truth to others, I want you to remember what I said today.

Of course, your ultimate self-realization means spreading the Truth to others, awakening their souls, and filling this world with wonderful people who have a heart of an angel. But missionary work—in other words, your ultimate self-realization—must be like the wind I just spoke of. Let it be like the wind. Do not let dust or sand get into it. As you carry out your activities, you might produce positive results, but you must not take credit for them. Self-assertiveness is not just different from what I mean by self-realization; it is the complete opposite of it. We do not need a wind that picks up sand and blows it on people. It is better not to have such wind in this world. It must be a wind that makes people happy. As the wind blows, it must bring a cool breeze that naturally fills people with joy. The wind exists to turn this world into heaven. The wind shall never blow for the sake of showing off its power. This is the checkpoint to keep in mind when you convey the Truth.

Please seek an infinitely selfless heart. The more you give love, the less noticeable you should be. Your seeds of love may bear fruits, but do not give yourself credit for them. Never seek appreciation from others. You are not giving love to others to win their gratitude. Love requires action to sustain itself as love. For love to remain love, it must be passed on from person to person. That is the mission of love. When love stops its activity, it will cease to exist. The love dwelling in your heart is not meant to stay still. It must constantly be active and flowing out. From now on, never limit the amount of love you supply. From now on, never limit yourself in spreading love. Do not restrain yourself. Do not bind yourself.

5

Without Love, Progress Is Dead

So far, I have spent a lot of time talking about love. Now, I must talk about progress as well. I said Hermes focused on lighting the candle in the heart of each person, one by one. But it certainly takes a tremendous amount of time and work to light the candle in each person's heart. That is why there is a need for progress.

Progress does not exist for its own sake. Progress exists to supply more love. Progress must serve love. Progress must empower love that gives and provide more and more people with opportunities to light the candle within them. Never forget this point.

In many cases, progress is something we can see. Take our activities, for example. The number of people attending my lectures is steadily increasing, and so are our membership and the number of offices, staff, and supporters. Our progress shows outwardly. This is how an organization expands. Even so, the point is that we do not make progress for the sake of progress itself. Without love, progress is dead. I must say so. Progress exists for the sake of realizing love. If progress will lead to the death of love, kill progress instead. Stop making progress. Progress must serve love. Progress is allowed on the condition that it gives limitless love to people. It is not a matter of love or progress. Love calls for progress. Progress is given as an opportunity to serve love further. Please know this.

So, the bigger and the more splendid your progress becomes, the more you must make sure the amount of your love does not decrease. For example, the more we expand our activities all over Japan, the more we must be determined not to reduce the love we put into them. Our love must not diminish even a bit—not even by a spoonful. If your progress is rapid, your supply of love must surpass it.

I dare say to each one of you: You may start your activities out of the wish to give love to many, but you may reach a point beyond your capability. You may sometimes be overwhelmed and fall. At such times, however, remember my words. When love dies, progress will be an empty shell. When love dies, progress will be an uninhabited house. It will be a pile of debris. It will be a ruined house. Yes, the one who lives in the building called "progress" must be the holy being named "love." You must never forget this.

6

Living with God's Will as Your Own

Do not simply be satisfied with outward appearances. Do not just be satisfied with earthly expansion. Have an abundance of love that surpasses earthly expansion. You must be that way. Otherwise, you are not a real human being.

Why do I say so? It has to do with our fundamental mission and the reason why we live on earth in a physical body. We are not born into this world merely for pleasure. We are not born on a whim. We are not born for mere show. We are not born to adorn ourselves. We are born on earth to create the Land of God's Love in this world. That is the reason why we are born on earth. It is natural for us to give love. That is because our very existence is made of great love.

Reflect on the decades of your life on earth. Reflect on the wrong thoughts that crossed your mind. Reflect on the many embarrassing deeds you would never want others to know about. Despite these thoughts and actions, you still have life. Do you realize what this means? You have been living with shameful thoughts and have done shameful acts during the decades of your life, but you still have life. Do you realize what this means? What does it mean that you still have a future? What does it mean that you still have hopes and dreams? You must know how great this love is that allows you to live now. Without realizing this love, you cannot be called human. You cannot be called a child of God. If you look back at your past, you will definitely realize that you have been given much more than you have given. If you fail to realize this, you have studied the Truth for nothing. You cannot say you see yourself rightly. Yes, you have been given so much.

Materialists and those who deny God and spirits are quick to laugh at the idea of reincarnation. They scoff at the idea that souls enter physical bodies to live in this world, cast off their shells like cicadas upon death, and spend their lives in heaven before they are reborn into this world. Indeed, this idea sounds absurd. It may sound ridiculous or wasteful. They may wonder why we must go through such a taxing process. However, that is love. It is God's love that allows us to live in this seemingly inefficient, wasteful, and roundabout cycle. Please know this love.

Love is not about efficiency. Love is not about rationality. Love is not about effectiveness. God keeps watch over your repeating seemingly wasteful lives or wasteful cycles without ever giving up on you. At the root of love lies God's patience. Now that we are aware of this truth, we must not stop love. We cannot stop love, just as we cannot stop the wind. Wind is no longer wind when it stops blowing. Like the wind, love ceases to exist when it stops blowing. If you are aware that you are being allowed to live, feel thankful for that, and are able to understand even a handful or a grain of God's Will, then keep blowing through the world without limit. Like the wind, be pure and clear. Be selfless and without vanity. Do not seek appreciation from others. You are given everything, so never seek praise from others or even from God.

Indeed, that is our mission. That is our work. Being alive means we must keep on giving love. That is why we cannot stop loving. We cannot stop loving because we are love itself, and our very existence—our souls—is an expression of love. Yes, we must start with "love that gives." And because we are human, we cannot master "love that gives" completely. Look at God, who is beyond humans. God is the embodiment of "love that gives"—the level we humans can never reach no matter how hard we try. God is a mass of love. God is love itself. God is the ultimate form of "love incarnate."

Now, everyone, do you understand the meaning of today's title, "The Ultimate Self-Realization"? There is no "ultimate" to the ultimate self-realization. Do you understand this paradox? The ultimate self-realization means to live with God's Will as your own. There is no ultimate to such a life. Unfortunately, even a nine-dimensional spirit cannot reach the ultimate as long as they live as a human. We must keep living in the midst of this endless, transparent sadness. We are such beings.

Even so, you must not think too much about the tears in your eyes. Your tears may sparkle like the Aegean Sea, but let them be the spiritual nourishment for those who see them. Do not think of them as your own. Let your tears be infinitely clear, blue, beautiful, and filled with light. Set off on the march of love and the march of light in this sacred sadness.

The ultimate self-realization means to constantly understand and grasp God's Will and to move forward, on and on, like the wind that keeps blowing. Imagine all of you becoming like the wind and blowing throughout the world. What a wonderful world it would be. How full of blessings and light this world would be. Please embrace the wind that came from me today. And I hope you, too, will blow like the wind without ever stopping. Thank you very much.

Afterword

For over 30 years, I have been doing endless and limitless work, as if I were counting the grains of sand in the Ganges River.

Now, the Laws I have preached are myself.

In this book, I kept the editing to a minimum so that you can truly relive my lectures that were given back then.

Here lie the passionate and powerful speeches of El Cantare in His youth.

Ryuho Okawa
Master & CEO of Happy Science Group
January 9, 2021

For a deeper understanding of
What Is Happy Science?
see other books below by Ryuho Okawa:

The Golden Laws [Tokyo, HS Press, 2015]

The Ten Principles from El Cantare Volume I [New York, IRH Press, 2021]

The Ten Principles from El Cantare Volume II [New York, IRH Press, 2022]

The Unhappiness Syndrome [New York, IRH Press, 2017]

The True Eightfold Path [New York, IRH Press, 2021]

The Essence of Buddha [New York, IRH Press, 2016]

ABOUT THE AUTHOR

Founder and CEO of Happy Science Group.

Ryuho Okawa was born on July 7th 1956, in Tokushima, Japan. After graduating from the University of Tokyo with a law degree, he joined a Tokyo-based trading house. While working at its New York headquarters, he studied international finance at the Graduate Center of the City University of New York. In 1981, he attained Great Enlightenment and became aware that he is El Cantare with a mission to bring salvation to all humankind.

In 1986, he established Happy Science. It now has members in 168 countries across the world, with more than 700 branches and temples as well as 10,000 missionary houses around the world.

He has given over 3,500 lectures (of which more than 150 are in English) and published over 3,100 books (of which more than 600 are Spiritual Interview Series), and many are translated into 41 languages. Along with *The Laws of the Sun* and *The Laws of Hell*, many of the books have become best sellers or million sellers. To date, Happy Science has produced 27 movies. The original story and original concept were given by the Executive Producer Ryuho Okawa. He has also composed music and written lyrics of over 450 pieces.

Moreover, he is the Founder of Happy Science University and Happy Science Academy (Junior and Senior High School), Founder and President of the Happiness Realization Party, Founder and Honorary Headmaster of Happy Science Institute of Government and Management, Founder of IRH Press Co., Ltd., and the Chairperson of NEW STAR PRODUCTION Co., Ltd. and ARI Production Co., Ltd.

BOOKS BY RYUHO OKAWA

Basic Teachings of Happy Science

The Ten Principles from El Cantare Volume I

Ryuho Okawa's First Lectures on His Basic Teachings

Paperback • 232 pages • $16.95
ISBN: 978-1-942125-85-3 (Dec. 15, 2021)

This book contains the historic lectures given on the first five principles of the Ten Principles of Happy Science from the author, Ryuho Okawa, who is revered as World Teacher. These lectures produced an enthusiastic fellowship in Happy Science Japan and became the foundation of the current global utopian movement. You can learn the essence of Okawa's teachings and the secret behind the rapid growth of the Happy Science movement in simple language.

The Ten Principles from El Cantare Volume II

Ryuho Okawa's First Lectures on His Wish to Save the World

Paperback • 272 pages • $16.95
ISBN: 978-1-942125-86-0 (May 3, 2022)

A sequel to *The Ten Principles from El Cantare Volume I*. Volume II reveals the Creator's three major inventions; the secret of the creation of human souls, the meaning of time, and 'happiness' as life's purpose. By reading this book, you can not only improve yourself but learn how to make differences in society and create an ideal, utopian world.

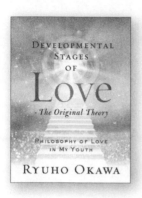

Developmental Stages of Love - The Original Theory

Philosophy of Love in My Youth

Hardcover • 200 pages • $17.95
ISBN: 978-1-942125-94-5 (Jun. 15, 2022)

This book is about author Ryuho Okawa's original philosophy of love which serves as the foundation of love in the chapter three of *The Laws of the Sun*. It consists of series of short essays authored during his age of 25 through 28 while he was working as a young promising business elite at an international trading company after attaining the Great Enlightenment in 1981. The developmental stages of love unites love and enlightenment, West and East, and bridges Christianity and Buddhism.

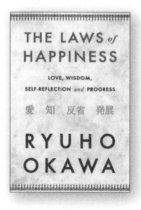

The Laws of Happiness

Love, Wisdom, Self-Reflection and Progress

Paperback • 264 pages • $16.95
ISBN: 978-1-942125-70-9 (Aug. 28, 2020)

Happiness is not found outside us; it is found within us. It is in how we think, how we look at our lives, and how we devote our hearts to the work we do. Discover how the Fourfold Path of Love, Wisdom, Self-Reflection and Progress create a life of sustainable happiness.

El Cantare Trilogy

The Laws Series is an annual volume of books that are comprised of Ryuho Okawa's lectures that function as universal guidance to all people. They are of various topics that were given in accordance with the changes that each year brings. *The Laws of the Sun*, the first publication of the laws series, ranked in the annual best-selling list in Japan in 1994. Since, the laws series' titles have ranked in the annual best-selling list every year for more than two decades, setting socio-cultural trends in Japan and around the world.

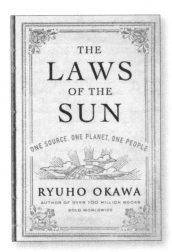

The Laws of the Sun

One Source, One Planet,
One People

Paperback • 288 pages • $15.95
ISBN: 978-1-942125-43-3 (Oct. 15, 2018)

IMAGINE IF YOU COULD ASK GOD why He created this world and what spiritual laws He used to shape us—and everything around us. If we could understand His designs and intentions, we could discover what our goals in life should be and whether our actions move us closer to those goals or farther away.

At a young age, a spiritual calling prompted Ryuho Okawa to outline what he innately understood to be universal truths for all humankind. In *The Laws of the Sun*, Okawa outlines these laws of the universe and provides a road map for living one's life with greater purpose and meaning. In this powerful book, Ryuho Okawa reveals the transcendent nature of consciousness and the secrets of our multidimensional universe and our place in it. By understanding the different stages of love and following the Buddhist Eightfold Path, he believes we can speed up our eternal process of development. *The Laws of the Sun* shows the way to realize true happiness—a happiness that continues from this world through the other.

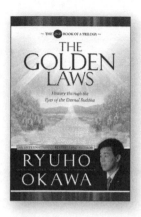

The Golden Laws

History through the Eyes of
the Eternal Buddha

E-book • 204 pages • $13.99
ISBN: 978-1-941779-82-8 (Sep. 24, 2015)

Throughout history, Great Guiding Spirits have been present on Earth in both the East and the West at crucial points in human history to further our spiritual development. *The Golden Laws* reveals how Divine Plan has been unfolding on Earth, and outlines 5,000 years of the secret history of humankind. Once we understand the true course of history, through past, present and into the future, we cannot help but become aware of the significance of our spiritual mission in the present age.

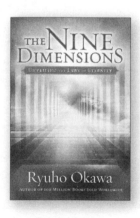

The Nine Dimensions

Unveiling the Laws of Eternity

Paperback • 168 pages • $15.95
ISBN: 978-0-982698-56-3 (Feb. 16, 2012)

This book is a window into the mind of our loving God, who designed this world and the vast, wondrous world of our afterlife as a school with many levels through which our souls learn and grow. When the religions and cultures of the world discover the truth of their common spiritual origin, they will be inspired to accept their differences, come together under faith in God, and build an era of harmony and peaceful progress on Earth.

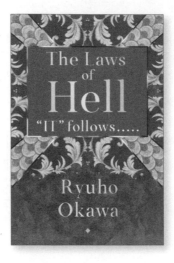

The Laws of Hell

"IT" follows .....

Paperback • 264 pages • $17.95
ISBN: 978-1-958655-04-7 (May 1, 2023)

Whether you believe it or not, the Spirit World and hell do exist. Currently, the Earth's population has exceeded 8 billion, and unfortunately, 1 in 2 people are falling to hell.

This book is a must-read at a time like this since more and more people are unknowingly heading to hell; the truth is, new areas of hell are being created, such as 'internet hell' and 'hell on earth.' Also, due to the widespread materialism, there is a sharp rise in the earthbound spirits wandering around earth because they have no clue about the Spirit World.

To stop hell from spreading and to save the souls of all human beings, the Spiritual Master, Ryuho Okawa has compiled vital teachings in this book. This publication marks his 3,100th book and is the one and only comprehensive Truth about the modern hell.

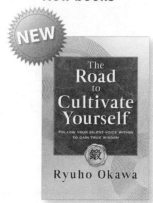

The Road to Cultivate Yourself

Follow Your Silent Voice Within to Gain True Wisdom

Paperback • 256 pages • $17.95
ISBN: 978-1-958655-05-4 (Jun. 22, 2023)

What is the ideal way of living when chaos and destruction are accelerated? This book offers unchanging Truth in the ever-changing world, such as the secrets to become more aware about the spiritual self and how to increase intellectual productivity amidst the rapid changes of the modern age. It is packed with Author Ryuho Okawa's crystallized wisdom of life.

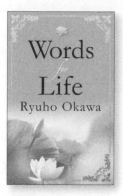

Words for Life

Paperback • 136 pages • $15.95
ISBN: 979-8-88727-089-7 (Mar. 16, 2023)

Ryuho Okawa has written over 3,100 books on various topics. To help readers find the teachings that are beneficial for them out of the extensive teachings, the author has written 100 phrases and put them together in this book. Inside you will find words of wisdom that will help you improve your mindset, change you into a more capable and insightful person, and lead you to live a meaningful and happy life.

The Challenge of Enlightenment

Now, Here, the New Dharma Wheel Turns

Paperback • 380 pages • $17.95
ISBN: 978-1-942125-92-1 (Dec. 20, 2022)

Buddha's teachings, a reflection of his eternal wisdom, are like a bamboo pole used to change the course of your boat in the rapid stream of the great river called life. By reading this book, your mind becomes clearer, learns to savor inner peace, and it will empower you to make profound life improvements.

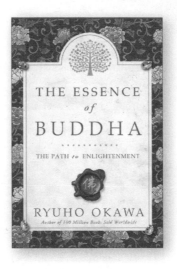

The Essence of Buddha

The Path to Enlightenment

Paperback • 208 pages • $14.95
ISBN: 978-1-942125-06-8 (Oct.1, 2016)

In this book, Ryuho Okawa imparts in simple and accessible language his wisdom about the essence of Shakyamuni Buddha's philosophy of life and enlightenment–teachings that have been inspiring people all over the world for over 2,500 years. By offering a new perspective on core Buddhist thoughts that have long been cloaked in mystique, Okawa brings these teachings to life for modern people. *The Essence of Buddha* distills a way of life that anyone can practice to achieve a life of self-growth, compassionate living, and true happiness.

The True Eightfold Path

Guideposts for Self-Innovation

Paperback • 256 pages • $16.95
ISBN: 978-1-942125-80-8 (Mar. 30, 2021)

This book explains how we can apply the Eightfold Path, one of the main pillars of Shakyamuni Buddha's teachings, as everyday guideposts in the modern-age to achieve self-innovation to live better and make positive changes in these uncertain times.

The Rebirth of Buddha

My Eternal Disciples, Hear My Words

Paperback • 280 pages • $17.95
ISBN: 978-1-942125-95-2 (Jul. 15, 2022)

These are the messages of Buddha who has returned to this modern age as promised to His eternal beloved disciples. They are in simple words and poetic style, yet contain profound messages. Once you start reading these passages, your soul will be replenished as the plant absorbs the water, and you will remember why you chose this era to be born into with Buddha. Listen to the voices of your Eternal Master and awaken to your calling.

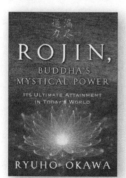

Rojin, Buddha's Mystical Power

Its Ultimate Attainment in Today's World

Paperback • 224 pages • $16.95
ISBN: 978-1-942125-82-2 (Sep. 24, 2021)

In this book, Ryuho Okawa has redefined the traditional Buddhist term *Rojin* and explained that in modern society it means the following: the ability for individuals with great spiritual powers to live in the world as people with common sense while using their abilities to the optimal level. This book will unravel the mystery of the mind and lead you to the path to enlightenment.

The New Genre of Spiritual Mystery Novel
- The Unknown Stigma Trilogy -

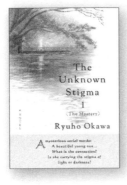

The Unknown Stigma 1 <The Mystery>

Hardcover • 192 pages • $17.95
ISBN: 978-1-942125-28-0 (Oct. 1, 2022)

The first spiritual mystery novel by Ryuho Okawa. It happened one early summer afternoon, in a densely wooded park in Tokyo: following a loud scream of a young woman, the alleged victim was found lying with his eyes rolled back and foaming at the mouth. But there was no sign of forced trauma, nor even a drop of blood. Then, similar murder cases continued one after another without any clues. Later, this mysterious serial murder case leads back to a young Catholic nun...

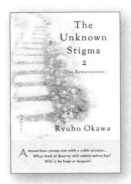

The Unknown Stigma 2 <The Resurrection>

Hardcover • 180 pages • $17.95
ISBN: 978-1-942125-31-0 (Nov. 1, 2022)

A sequel to *The Unknown Stigma 1 <The Mystery>* by Ryuho Okawa. After an extraordinary spiritual experience, a young, mysterious Catholic nun is now endowed with a new, noble mission. What kind of destiny will she face? Will it be hope or despair that awaits her? The story develops into a turn of events that no one could ever have anticipated. Are you ready to embrace its shocking ending?

The Unknown Stigma 3 <The Universe>

Hardcover • 184 pages • $17.95
ISBN: 978-1-958655-00-9 (Dec. 1, 2022)

In this astonishing sequel to the first two installments of *The Unknown Stigma*, the protagonist journeys through the universe and encounters a mystical world unknown to humankind. Discover what awaits her beyond this mysterious world.

Other Recommended Titles

The Unhappiness Syndrome
28 Habits of Unhappy People (and How to Change Them)

The Miracle of Meditation
Opening Your Life to Peace, Joy and the Power Within

Twiceborn
My Early Thoughts that Revealed My True Mission

The Laws of Success
A Spiritual Guide to Turning Your Hopes into Reality

Invincible Thinking
An Essential Guide for a Lifetime of
Growth, Success, and Triumph

The Laws of Secret
Awaken to This New World and Change Your Life

The Challenge of the Mind
An Essential Guide to Buddha's Teachings:
Zen, Karma and Enlightenment

The Power of Basics
Introduction to Modern Zen Life
of Calm, Spirituality and Success

Spiritual World 101
A guide to a spiritually happy life

For a complete list of books, visit okawabooks.com

WHO IS EL CANTARE?

El Cantare means "the Light of the Earth." He is the Supreme God of the Earth who has been guiding humankind since the beginning of Genesis, and He is the Creator of the universe. He is whom Jesus called Father and Muhammad called Allah, and is *Ame-no-Mioya-Gami*, Japanese Father God. Different parts of El Cantare's core consciousness have descended to Earth in the past, once as Alpha and another as Elohim. His branch spirits, such as Shakyamuni Buddha and Hermes, have descended to Earth many times and helped to flourish many civilizations. To unite various religions and to integrate various fields of study in order to build a new civilization on Earth, a part of the core consciousness has descended to Earth as Master Ryuho Okawa.

Alpha is a part of the core consciousness of El Cantare who descended to Earth around 330 million years ago. Alpha preached Earth's Truths to harmonize and unify Earth-born humans and space people who came from other planets.

Elohim is a part of the core consciousness of El Cantare who descended to Earth around 150 million years ago. He gave wisdom, mainly on the differences of light and darkness, good and evil.

Ame-no-Mioya-Gami (Japanese Father God) is the Creator God and the Father God who appears in the ancient literature, *Hotsuma Tsutae*. It is believed that He descended on the foothills of Mt. Fuji about 30,000 years ago and built the Fuji dynasty, which is the root of the Japanese civilization. With justice as the central pillar, Ame-no-Mioya-Gami's teachings spread to ancient civilizations of other countries in the world.

Shakyamuni Buddha was born as a prince into the Shakya Clan in India around 2,600 years ago. When he was 29 years old, he renounced the world and sought enlightenment. He later attained Great Enlightenment and founded Buddhism.

Hermes is one of the 12 Olympian gods in Greek mythology, but the spiritual Truth is that he taught the teachings of love and progress around 4,300 years ago that became the origin of the current Western civilization. He is a hero that truly existed.

Ophealis was born in Greece around 6,500 years ago and was the leader who took an expedition to as far as Egypt. He is the God of miracles, prosperity, and arts, and is known as Osiris in the Egyptian mythology.

Rient Arl Croud was born as a king of the ancient Incan Empire around 7,000 years ago and taught about the mysteries of the mind. In the heavenly world, he is responsible for the interactions that take place between various planets.

Thoth was an almighty leader who built the golden age of the Atlantic civilization around 12,000 years ago. In the Egyptian mythology, he is known as God Thoth.

Ra Mu was a leader who built the golden age of the civilization of Mu around 17,000 years ago. As a religious leader and a politician, he ruled by uniting religion and politics.

ABOUT HAPPY SCIENCE

Happy Science is a religious group founded on the faith in El Cantare who is the God of the Earth, and the Creator of the universe. The essence of human beings is the soul that was created by God, and we all are children of God. God is our true parent, so in our souls we have a fundamental desire to "believe in God, love God, and get closer to God." And, we can get closer to God by living with God's Will as our own. In Happy Science, we call this the "Exploration of Right Mind." More specifically, it means to practice the Fourfold Path, which consists of "Love, Wisdom, Self-Reflection, and Progress."

Love: Love means "love that gives," or mercy. God hopes for the happiness of all people. Therefore, living with God's Will as our own means to start by practicing "love that gives."

Wisdom: God's love is boundless. It is important to learn various Truths in order to understand the heart of God.

Self-Reflection: Once you learn the heart of God and the difference between His mind and yours, you should strive to bring your own mind closer to the mind of God— that process is called self-reflection. Self-reflection also includes meditation and prayer.

Progress: Since God hopes for the happiness of all people, you should also make progress in your love, and make an effort to realize utopia in which everyone in your society, country, and eventually all humankind can become happy.

As we practice this Fourfold Path, our souls will advance toward God step by step. That is when we can attain real happiness— our souls' desire to get closer to God comes true.

In Happy Science, we conduct activities to make ourselves happy through belief in Lord El Cantare, and to spread this faith to the world and bring happiness to all. We welcome you to join our activities!

We hold events and activities to help you practice the Fourfold Path at our branches, temples, missionary centers and missionary houses

Love: We hold various volunteering activities. Our members conduct missionary work together as the greatest practice of love.

Wisdom: We offer our comprehensive books collection, many of which bookstores do not have available. In addition, we give out numerous opportunities such as seminars or book clubs to learn the Truth.

Self-Reflection: We offer opportunities to polish your mind through self-reflection, meditation, and prayer. There are many cases in which members have experienced improvement in their human relationships by changing their own minds.

Progress: We also offer seminars to enhance your power of influence. Because it is also important to do well at work to make society better, we hold seminars to improve your work and management skills.

"The True Words Spoken By Buddha"

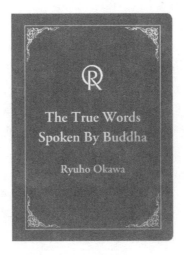

The True Words Spoken By Buddha is an English sutra given directly from the spirit of Shakyamuni Buddha, who is a part of Master Ryuho Okawa's subconscious. The words in this sutra are not of a mere human being but are the words of God or Buddha sent directly from the ninth dimension, which is the highest realm of the Earth's Spirit World.

The True Words Spoken By Buddha is an essential sutra for us to connect and live with God or Buddha's Will as our own.

MEMBERSHIPS

MEMBERSHIP

If you would like to know more about Happy Science, please consider becoming a member. Those who pledge to believe in Lord El Cantare and wish to learn more can join us.

When you become a member, you will receive the following sutra books: *The True Words Spoken By Buddha*, *Prayer to the Lord* and *Prayer to Guardian and Guiding Spirits*.

DEVOTEE MEMBER

If you would like to learn the teachings of Happy Science and walk the path of faith, become a Devotee member who pledges devotion to the Three Treasures, which are Buddha, Dharma, and Sangha. Buddha refers to Lord El Cantare, Master Ryuho Okawa. Dharma refers to Master Ryuho Okawa's teachings. Sangha refers to Happy Science. Devoting to the Three Treasures will let your Buddha-nature shine, and you will enter the path to attain true freedom of the mind.

Becoming a devotee means you become Buddha's disciple. You will discipline your mind and act to bring happiness to society.

✉ **EMAIL** OR ☎ **PHONE CALL**
Please see the contact information page.

🔊 **ONLINE** (member.happy-science.org/signup/)

CONTACT INFORMATION

Happy Science is a worldwide organization with branches and temples around the globe. For a comprehensive list, visit the worldwide directory at happy-science.org. The following are some of our main Happy Science locations:

UNITED STATES AND CANADA

New York
79 Franklin St., New York, NY 10013, USA
Phone: 1-212-343-7972
Fax: 1-212-343-7973
Email: ny@happy-science.org
Website: happyscience-usa.org

New Jersey
66 Hudson St., #2R, Hoboken, NJ 07030, USA
Phone: 1-201-313-0127
Email: nj@happy-science.org
Website: happyscience-usa.org

Chicago
2300 Barrington Rd., Suite #400,
Hoffman Estates, IL 60169, USA
Phone: 1-630-937-3077
Email: chicago@happy-science.org
Website: happyscience-usa.org

Florida
5208 8th St., Zephyrhills, FL 33542, USA
Phone: 1-813-715-0000
Fax: 1-813-715-0010
Email: florida@happy-science.org
Website: happyscience-usa.org

Atlanta
1874 Piedmont Ave., NE Suite 360-C
Atlanta, GA 30324, USA
Phone: 1-404-892-7770
Email: atlanta@happy-science.org
Website: happyscience-usa.org

San Francisco
525 Clinton St.
Redwood City, CA 94062, USA
Phone & Fax: 1-650-363-2777
Email: sf@happy-science.org
Website: happyscience-usa.org

Los Angeles
1590 E. Del Mar Blvd., Pasadena,
CA 91106, USA
Phone: 1-626-395-7775
Fax: 1-626-395-7776
Email: la@happy-science.org
Website: happyscience-usa.org

Orange County
16541 Gothard St. Suite 104
Huntington Beach, CA 92647
Phone: 1-714-659-1501
Email: oc@happy-science.org
Website: happyscience-usa.org

San Diego
7841 Balboa Ave. Suite #202
San Diego, CA 92111, USA
Phone: 1-626-395-7775
Fax: 1-626-395-7776
E-mail: sandiego@happy-science.org
Website: happyscience-usa.org

Hawaii
Phone: 1-808-591-9772
Fax: 1-808-591-9776
Email: hi@happy-science.org
Website: happyscience-usa.org

Kauai
3343 Kanakolu Street, Suite 5
Lihue, HI 96766, USA
Phone: 1-808-822-7007
Fax: 1-808-822-6007
Email: kauai-hi@happy-science.org
Website: happyscience-usa.org

Toronto
845 The Queensway
Etobicoke, ON M8Z 1N6, Canada
Phone: 1-416-901-3747
Email: toronto@happy-science.org
Website: happy-science.ca

Vancouver
#201-2607 East 49th Avenue,
Vancouver, BC, V5S 1J9, Canada
Phone: 1-604-437-7735
Fax: 1-604-437-7764
Email: vancouver@happy-science.org
Website: happy-science.ca

INTERNATIONAL

Tokyo
1-6-7 Togoshi, Shinagawa,
Tokyo, 142-0041, Japan
Phone: 81-3-6384-5770
Fax: 81-3-6384-5776
Email: tokyo@happy-science.org
Website: happy-science.org

London
3 Margaret St.
London, W1W 8RE United Kingdom
Phone: 44-20-7323-9255
Fax: 44-20-7323-9344
Email: eu@happy-science.org
Website: www.happyscience-uk.org

Sydney
516 Pacific Highway, Lane Cove North,
2066 NSW, Australia
Phone: 61-2-9411-2877
Fax: 61-2-9411-2822
Email: sydney@happy-science.org

Sao Paulo
Rua. Domingos de Morais 1154,
Vila Mariana, Sao Paulo SP
CEP 04010-100, Brazil
Phone: 55-11-5088-3800
Email: sp@happy-science.org
Website: happyscience.com.br

Jundiai
Rua Congo, 447, Jd. Bonfiglioli
Jundiai-CEP, 13207-340, Brazil
Phone: 55-11-4587-5952
Email: jundiai@happy-science.org

Seoul
74, Sadang-ro 27-gil,
Dongjak-gu, Seoul, Korea
Phone: 82-2-3478-8777
Fax: 82-2-3478-9777
Email: korea@happy-science.org

Taipei
No. 89, Lane 155, Dunhua N. Road,
Songshan District, Taipei City 105, Taiwan
Phone: 886-2-2719-9377
Fax: 886-2-2719-5570
Email: taiwan@happy-science.org

Taichung
No. 146, Minzu Rd., Central Dist.,
Taichung City 400001, Taiwan (R.O.C.)
Phone: 886-4-22233777
Email: taichung@happy-science.org

Kuala Lumpur
No 22A, Block 2, Jalil Link Jalan Jalil Jaya
2, Bukit Jalil 57000,
Kuala Lumpur, Malaysia
Phone: 60-3-8998-7877
Fax: 60-3-8998-7977
Email: malaysia@happy-science.org
Website: happyscience.org.my

Kathmandu
Kathmandu Metropolitan City,
Ward No. 15, Ring Road, Kimdol,
Sitapaila Kathmandu, Nepal
Phone: 977-1-537-2931
Email: nepal@happy-science.org

Kampala
Plot 877 Rubaga Road, Kampala
P.O. Box 34130 Kampala, UGANDA
Email: uganda@happy-science.org

ABOUT IRH PRESS USA

IRH Press USA Inc. was founded in 2013 as an affiliated firm of IRH Press Co., Ltd. Based in New York, the press publishes books in various categories including spirituality, religion, and self-improvement and publishes books by Ryuho Okawa, the author of over 100 million books sold worldwide. For more information, visit okawabooks.com.

Follow us on:

f Facebook: Okawa Books   ◎ Instagram: OkawaBooks

▶ Youtube: Okawa Books   🐦 Twitter: Okawa Books

𝓟 Pinterest: Okawa Books   g Goodreads: Ryuho Okawa

—— **NEWSLETTER** ——

To receive book related news, promotions and events, please subscribe to our newsletter below.

🔗 irhpress.com/pages/subscribe

 —— **AUDIO / VISUAL MEDIA** ——

YOUTUBE   **PODCAST**

Introduction of Ryuho Okawa's titles; topics ranging from self-help, current affairs, spirituality, religion, and the universe.